GLOBALIZATION
OF URBANITY

USUM—*Urban Systems and Urban Models* is a research project that forms part of the SCPA —Swiss Cooperation Programme in Architecture. The principal objective of the SCPA is to promote and establish cooperation between Swiss higher education architectural schools in terms of research, as well as of teaching at the undergraduate and postgraduate levels. It is thus in line with the main strategic objectives of Swiss research and higher education policy, where cooperation in the field of architecture is explicitly requested by the BFI message 2008 —2011. The programme comprises the USI—Università della Svizzera Italiana, the two Federal Institutes of Technology in Zurich (ETH Zurich) and in Lausanne (EPF Lausanne), as well as the University of Applied Sciences of Southern Switzerland (SUPSI). The programme focuses on four main areas in architecture research and education: urban studies, urban design, environment and landscape; theory and history of architecture; renovation and restoration, construction and building technologies. More specifically, USUM's partners are the institutes of Swiss schools of Architecture involved in urban studies, which are i.CUP—institute for Contemporary Urban Project / AAM—USI, Chôros Laboratory / SAR / ENAC / EPFL, Faculty of Architecture ETH Zurich.

▼

The USUM—Urban Systems and Urban Models research project is a study of the contemporary city and urban space which adopts a systemic perspective for approaching the urban complexity and the nature of urban / public space in the era of globalization.

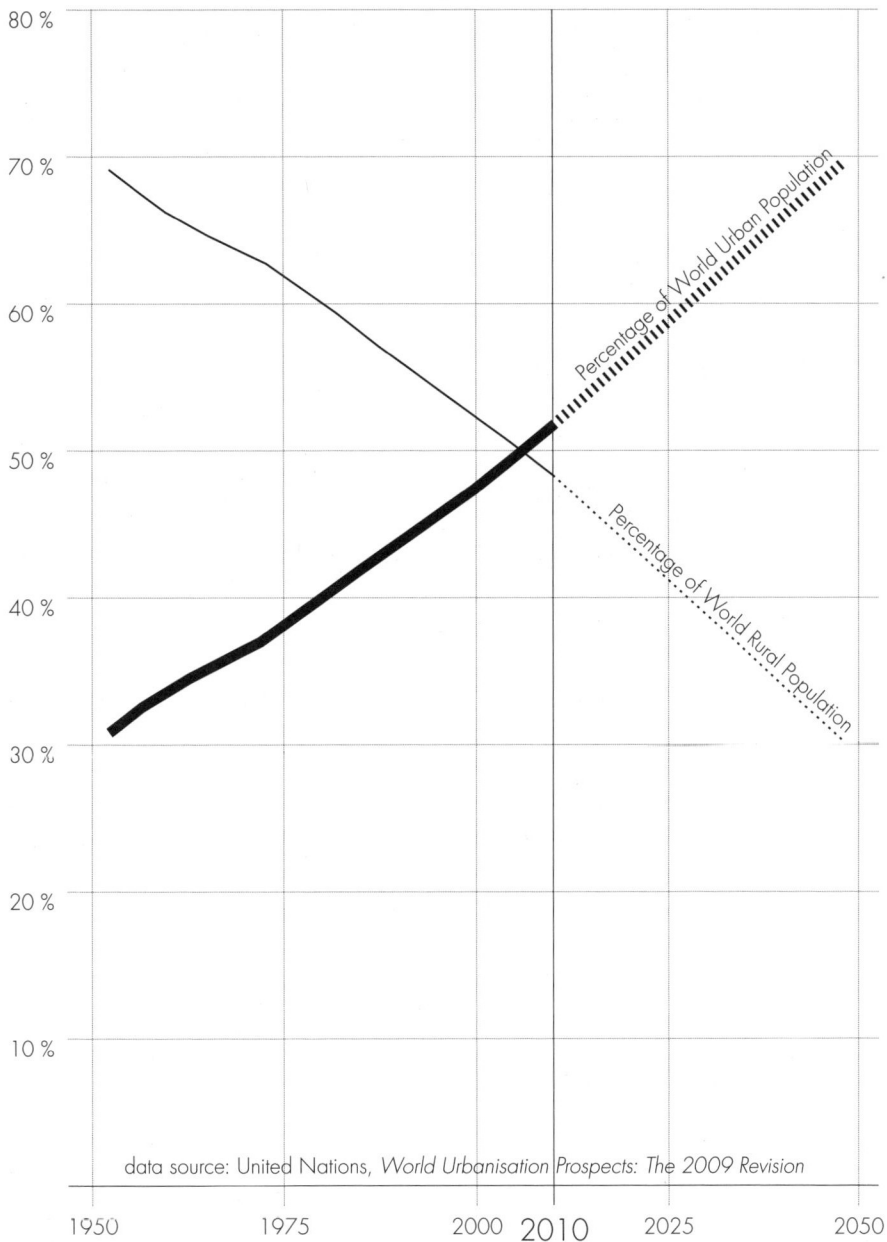

80 %

70 %

Percentage of World Urban Population

60 %

50 %

Percentage of World Rural Population

40 %

30 %

20 %

10 %

data source: United Nations, *World Urbanisation Prospects: The 2009 Revision*

1950   1975   2000 2010   2025   2050

Globalization of Urbanity

Recently, the process of urbanisation has radically mutated. The new contemporary parameters, like informational technology, the neotertiary economic sector, and the globalization process require a major revision of the urban models with which we operate, and which are still a reflection of the old paradigms resulting from the industrial revolution, the mechanical technology and the single-scale nation-state. Urban space is more and more an open, dynamic, and comprehensive system, which makes possible to identify different urban realities inside the same city. A new language and new theoretical approaches must be developed in order to understand present-day urbanisation processes. As a consequence, the USUM—Urban Systems and Urban Models research project aims at investigating present-day urbanisation processes in their actual complexity. Two main issue in particular have been addressed by the USUM research project: (1) the development of a multi-scalar and comparative approach for empirical research in the urban field both in socio-political and environmental terms; (2) the analysis of the transformation of urbanisation processes and urban / public space.

In this context, the USUM research project has considered since the very beginning the cooperation issue among the institutes involved as a concrete challenge to address with innovative and ambitious ways. The three partners of the research have decided to focus on the globalization of urbanity from their own research experience and perspective. As a consequence, the definition of three main WP—Work Packages has been intended to clearly separate and distinguish the different approaches and to ensure that every research team was able to deepen its own research area while cooperating and exchanging knowledge:

WP1. **Urban systems in the global urbanisation era**
Urban metabolism studies as global urbanisation agenda
resp. Prof. Josep Acebillo (i.CUP, USI AAM)

WP2. **Patterns and pathways of global urbanisation**
Comparative analysis on world urbanisation processes on a large scale
resp. Prof. Dr. Christian Schmid (Faculty of Architecture, ETHZ)

WP3. **Urban / public spaces in the global urbanisation era**
Comparative analysis of world urban spaces on a medium scale
resp. Prof. Dr. Jacques Lévy (SAR / Chôros, EPFL)

Fluctuations in population, in mobility, and in natural resources and energy, as well as fluctuations in the intensity of spatial configurations, are to be found in contemporary urban spaces as a result of their functional indefiniteness. These new parameters turn urban space into an open, dynamic, comprehensive system, which makes possible to identify various, proliferating cities within the same city. Even if the classic process of urbanisation as the transfer of a rural population into morphologically urban spaces is still in progress—as can be seen, for instance, in the dramatic move of hundreds of millions of people towards Chinese cities— the process of urbanisation has changed fundamentally in recent years.

Urbanisation has become relative.

It consists of a sort of injection of urbanity into already urbanized areas, whatever the appearance of their landscape may be. What is needed is a major revision of the current urban theses, that still reflect the old paradigms which emerged from the Industrial Revolution, and that are characterized by mechanical technology and the single-scale nation-state. In a full-time post-Fordist, digital, individual-oriented, integrally urbanised and globalised world, the way in which cities develop is still waiting to be established. A new language and a new theoretical approach must be developed in order to understand and drive present-day urbanisation processes.

In parallel with the three workpackages, many cooperative activities have been implemented, among which didactical cooperation, PhD researches, and a Summer School. In particular, the 3-days long Summer School, held in Lugano, was an interesting moment of confrontation in term of knowledge and the grow of a new perception of the globalization of urbanity. In particular, I hope that this cooperative attitude among researcher working in the fields of Urban studies will be reinforced in the future, in particular through the development of the PhD Thesis that are directed by the partners of the project within the USUM framework.

▼

Globalization of Urbanity is a compilation of the proceedings of the 2010 USUM Summer School organized by i.CUP—institute for Contemporary Urban Project as part of the cooperative research project USUM—Urban Systems and Urban Models.

Marcello Martinoni.
USUM coordinator-secretary,
Accademia di architettura—USI, Mendrisio

The i.CUP—institute for Contemporary Urban Project is the institute, directed by Prof. Arch. Josep Acebillo and coordinated by Arch. Enrico Sassi, within which this book has been produced. It is part of the Accademia di architettura—USI, Mendrisio.
While not denying the subjectivity of the territorial analysis, the aim of i.CUP is to promote objective and scientific territorial studies in order to react to the widespread misconception which fosters a solely aesthetic understanding of the territory. In order to deal with such a complex phenomenon, which involves natural and rural systems as well as the city, i.CUP bases its activities on projects and studies, especially in the field of mapping and strategic planning, system analysis and development, and urban infrastructures and architectural design, often adopting a transdisciplinary approach.

GLOBALIZATION OF URBANITY

Piero Martinoli, USI president

Summer School Opening.
Dear Professor Acebillo, Professor Schmid, Professor Lévy,
dear organizers, distinguished guests, and colleagues,
welcome to Università della Svizzera Italiana and to
the *Globalization of Urbanity* Summer School.
We are very pleased to host our colleagues from
the Faculty of Architecture of the ETH Zurich and
the Chôros Laboratory of EPFL, who work with the
i.CUP—institute for Contemporary Urban Project of the
Accademia di architettura in Mendrisio on the *Urban
Systems and Urban Models* project as part of the
Swiss cooperation program in architecture promoted
by the CUS. This forum offers an unparalleled opportunity to share knowledge and expand the discussions
regarding the today's cities, as well as the future of
urban areas.
Since Le Corbusier's decisive influence on modern architecture in the past century, metropolitan areas have undergone tremendous changes, as has the field of architecture. In the most recent issue of ETH *Globe magazine*,

Professor Eichler, President of ETH Zurich, points out how urban planning has become a multi-disciplinary field, transcending the borders of mere faculties—and I entirely agree! It can become an attractive and competitive field for both Swiss universities and Swiss firms, and your contributions during this Summer School can certainly be considered a national asset. You are here in a spirit of synergy, embracing the concept of adaptability to the forces of globalization: from rapid urbanisation to the opening up of borders, the implications are quite significant. Meanwhile, we are faced with the havoc caused by reckless energy consumption, which alters landscapes before our very eyes, coupled with rising temperatures and climate changes that demand structural modifications and retro-fitting of our buildings.

To quote Rem Koolhaas, a contemporary Dutch architect and Harvard professor who focuses on globalization, "the areas of consensus shift unbelievably fast; the bubbles of certainty are constantly exploding". The speed of change is the greatest challenge and, as he states, "increasingly, there is a discrepancy between the acceleration of culture and the continuing slowness of architecture." This is "the true challenge".

Indeed, what can be done when demand for urban space in places such as China exceeds the supply of architects and planners, and when the megacities of Asia and South America continue to sprawl outwards? Perhaps we can draw inspiration from our colleagues, for instance from experimental work by ETH scientists on urban systems, such as that of a "New Energy Self-Sufficient Town" outside the Ethiopian capital, which has the potential to efficiently transform suburbia.

I hope that the international and collaborative atmosphere of our Campus will inspire your work. USI will soon be embarking upon its fifteenth academic year. The number of students in our four faculties (Architecture, Communication, Economics and Informatics) is growing at a regular annual rate of roughly 7%. Today we

Piero Martinoli

have over 2,700 students, 62% of whom are from abroad, making USI the most international university in Switzerland. In this sense, USI is also an example of the movement of people and of impressive growth.

Before concluding, let me offer my sincere thanks to my colleagues of the i.CUP—institute for Contemporary Urban Project and, in particular, to Marcello Martinoni, Enrico Sassi and Monica Bancalà for the energy they have invested in organizing this event.May the Summer School session be a source of new ideas, with impact not only upon the participants themselves, but also on the more global context.

Josep Acebillo, was Professor at ETSAB, the School of
Architecture of Barcelona, from 1975 to 2000; Visiting Professor in
1997 at the School of Architecture, Yale University; Visiting Professor
in 2002 at the Graduate School of Design, Harvard University;
Visiting Professor in 2005/06 at the Department of Architecture
of NUS—National University of Singapore. Professor since 2001,
he was Dean of the Accademia di architettura—Università della
Svizzera Italiana, Mendrisio from 2003 to 2007. In 2008 he
cofounded the BiArch—Barcelona institute of Architecture, an
institution for post-graduate education and research in architecture
and urban studies. Since 1981, with various posts, he has been
a driving force behind the urban transformation of the city of
Barcelona: as Director of Urban Projects of the City of Barcelona
from 1981 to 1987; Technical Director of the Olympic Holding from
1988 to 1993; Chief Architect of the City of Barcelona from 1999
to 2002; CEO and Director since 1993 of the Barcelona Regional
Metropolitan Agency, which received the Special European Prize in
Urbanism 1997/98. For his contribution to the urban transformation
of Barcelona he was awarded the "Barcelona 1992" Honorific
Medal by the Barcelona Local Council and the 1999 Gold Medal
of Architecture, RIBA—Royal Institute of British Architects. Under
the urban leadership of Josep Acebillo, the city of Barcelona has
received worldwide recognition for its position in international
architecture and was awarded the 1990 Prince of Wales Prize in
Urban Design. In 2007 he founded the architectural office AUS—
Architecture & Urban Systems while today he is partner of the AS—
Archtectural Systems office, a firm which develops projects ranging
from architecture to urban design.

New global urban conditions. Good morning,
authorities, colleagues, Prof. Levy, Prof. Schmid and
all the friends here with us for these three days of lec-
tures and debate on the *Globalization of Urbanity*.
We have been working for the past year on the
concept of *Urban Models and Urban Systems* in the
context of a cooperation between the three schools
of architecture operating in Switzerland. After an
intense year of work, I think now is the best moment
to stop and examine the results so far in order to
check not only the perspectives of our project but also
the perspectives for urban investigation in the coming
future too.

1.
New Global Urban Conditions. Changes in the human
condition must be interpreted and translated into urban
theories and into architecture. In particular, with regard
to their recent but crucial innovations, I consider the

economical, technological and governmental conditions as crucial aspects to be evaluated for rethinking urban theories. In fact, throughout history, when these have changed, urban theories have changed too.
In the nineteenth century, agriculture disappeared as the dominant form of economical production in favour of the industrial one; new technologies appeared, especially for transport (i.e. rail systems, etc...); the most of the States that we know today came into existence. Within this evolutionary context, people like Thomas Jefferson, Ildefons Cerdà, and later Le Corbusier and Ludwig Hilberseimer, created the basis for what we consider modern urbanism, a form of urban theory absolutely different from any other before advanced. This transition, which occupied the second half of the nineteenth century and the first half of the twentieth, is what I call the *Urban Turn One*.
At the end of the twentieth century we have started to face again transformations in the economical, technological and governmental conditions: if in the nineteenth century agriculture declined in favour of industry, nowadays industry has declined in favour of a "neotertiary" economy; if heavy infrastructures began to be introduced into our lives during the nineteenth century, today the immaterial infrastructures which correspond to the new dimension of IT (the Internet, Wi-Fi technologies, etc...) are entering our life; if the nineteenth century witnessed the establishment of national governments, today supranational organizations are progressively increasing their governmental importance in the context of globalization. I think that the complex characterized by such emergent conditions—neotertiary economy, IT technologies, globalization—should be reclaimed as the *Urban Turn Two*.
In the light of this, today I think architects and urbanists—as it happened in the nineteenth century—must change their point of view: we need new theories, new ways of analyzing an urban question which is

Josep Acebillo

no longer what we were used to. Unfortunately this is not yet happening and, at the same time, it is not so clear that we need to make it happen.

In fact, while focusing such interrogatives, I'm pessimistic not because of the possibility to answer them but because of the present ways of teaching in the faculties of architecture of the entire world, where theory has been recently reduced to a limited moment exactly when the opposite would have been required. Because of this, I have almost no chance to explain to my students what phenomena are taking place within the city, simply because no scientific theoretical knowledge is given to or requested by them. But today, unfortunately, it is impossible to do anything in the urban space without using some convenient mathematic theory...

I have therefore reasons to consider that we are losing the possibility to re-drive reality towards a more inhabitable future, which is exactly the opposite of what happened in the *Urban Turn One* when Ildefons Cerdà was able to theoretically envision and to project an urban grid suitable for that today's form of individual mobility which at the time still had to come. With such precedents, I think that I should recall, to all architects, as well as to students, assistants, professor or practitioners of the urban world, our responsibilities in the current context of urban question transformation.

The Postfordist Transition. I consider some "vectors" absolutely relevant for framing the specificities of the contemporary urban question. They are: the *acceleration* of human processes, spurred by the increasing speed that the new technologies permit; the *socio-cultural diversity*, consequence of the multinational migration fluxes; and a new *ecologic approach*, that is transmitting to the general audience the metabolic consequence of urban transformations.

Here I will address the first one in particular. Today, according to Marc Augè, the incredible acceleration of our lives is implying an excess of time, of space, and of individualism. Absolutely true according to my personal experience: yesterday I was in Barcelona and today I'm here in Lugano. I commute twice a week, extending my capacities while interacting with larger and larger portions of the global territory but running the risk of losing a certain identity.

Concerning this loss of identity that *acceleration* implies, we can also consider the evolution of advanced economies in their progressive detachment from territorial contingencies: in Spain, for example, at the beginning of the twentieth century the productive proportion of the primary, secondary and tertiary sectors—agriculture, industries and services—was 49%, 24%, and 27% while at the end of the last century it was 5%, 30%, and 65%, which obviously promotes an isotropic vision of the territory.

This delocalization of life has unfortunately implied a sort of indolence to re-new territorial theories, an indolence well represented by the fact that what has animated the city of the last twenty years can be summed up in the FIRE acronym, which is Finance,

Insurance, Real-Estate and Enterprise. Not by chance, in the last ten years all the urban theoreticians have been busy in socio-economical and financial readings! In a way, the urban crisis in which we are embroiled today is therefore a direct result of the financial crisis we are suffering: if finance is saturated and we cannot continue to imagine that financial ideas will play a dominant role in urban development, today what was the FIRE of our cities is simply disappearing.

Urban Aporias: A Missed Opportunity. In this context of the FIRE paradigm, the urbanistic discipline of the last twenty years has been developing in a form of ideological crisis characterized by certain "excesses".

Josep Acebillo

These are negative not becasue of their "content" but rather because of their hypertrophy, which has led to some irresolvable issues - or urban aporias - especially in terms of the following:

1. *False historicism.* With the false pretext of historical references, history has become a justification for camouflaging real problems and provoking proactive sclerosis and counter-innovation, thus prompting the spread of a conservative approach. In fact, if reference to history as an ineluctable cultural context is one thing, another one is the substitution of an innovatory perspective with a narrow vision, solely historical, which "freezes" any perspective of change.

2. *Excess of simulation and epidermic approach.* The tendency to simulate reality has masked the difference between truth and deceit, between real and imaginary, and has prompted confusion between actuality and desire. The substitution of a structural territorial theory by a banal form of "landscaping", as a condition for urban intervention, is an unfortunate example of this excess. The point is that today it is not necessary to go back to "dirty realism", neither to doubt on the potentialities of building envelopes, rather to deepen the understanding of territorial dynamics in the light of their contemporary conditions.

3. *Excess of iconic references.* Viewing architecture as a marketing process has led to the predominance of iconic buildings that fail to interact with their surrounding sites as well as to architectural forms gratuitous and dysfunctional. On the erroneous basis of a "generic city", which has spurred a sort of carelessness for the context, it has been in fact produced an excess of "homogenization", the compensation of which has been achieved with iconic *ex-abruptos* that finally belittle urban form.

In any case, this focus on urban icons has leaded away from the Vitruvian virtues of *utilitas, firmitas, venustas*, and thus to urban trivialization.

4. Confusion between "goods"and "rights".
Even if the city is the most appropriate field for the development of trade and exchange, this fact doesn't imply its very identification with trade. In fact, if such "analogy" is abused, the "right to the city" as a territory of democracy and social justice can be put under threaten, the right to housing can be layed on the line because of cost, the "new urban commons" (public space and facilities) subjected to pay-tolls which reduce their necessary accessibility...

5. Insecurity syndrom. Even if specialists claim that today we live in the most secure period ever in history, it is progressively circulating a feeling of insecurity around us, which consequences deeply conditions our life and threatens our privacy. An "invisible panopticism" is in fact under production in our cities, but not in architectural forms, rather in sophisticated technologies of surveillance (i.e. the proliferation of CCTV cameras, the use of electronic cash trading as matter of fiscal control, etc...) which reach our intimacy as much as produce barriers breaking up the public-ness of the urban territory. This unattractive disciplinary approaches must be completely re-considered in order to permit new options for post-crisis urban models. The architecture and the urbanistic discipline of the last twenty years has unfortunately not been able to re-drive urban thesis, ending up in a trivialization of the urban project that clearly missed the opportunity to configure that *Urban Turn Two* which is now reclaimed.
Today only the last of the four FIRE components remains at our disposal: the human capacity for Enterprise. For this reason, education - and higher education in particular - is more important than ever: confronting the contemporary crisis we need not to forget that it is in man and in its networked capacities, and not in the territory by itself, that we shall find new power and opportunities.

Josep Acebillo

2.

New Urban Complexity. I sum up this idea of mine in the slogan *Networks for Land*: in order to develop further, I think networks and relationships between people will be far more important than any territorial constraint. More precisely, by this centrality of networks I do not mean a necessity to disregard the actual territory or to further expand urbanisation with its institutions

(☞ fig.1) and infrastructures, but rather the necessity to actually understand the city in its networked complexity. A new approach to the actuality of urban complexity must be developed from an acknowledgement of such.

The urban complexity has been progressively increasing since the advent of the *Urban Turn One*. Now, in the contemporary globalization of urbanity, the emergence of a possible thermodynamic approach to appreciate urban processes in the light of their networked condition can be considered the last achievement of this increasing complexity. Today we can understand a city "as an open and complex system" and because of this we can read its behaviour through system theory parameters like *stability, irreversibility* and *fluctuations*.

Well beyond from simply being a perceptive tension, complexity is in fact a mathematical concept relating to system theory and especially to the concrete reality of dissipative structures: all the cities in the world are systemic structures, distinguished by a clear tendency towards a state of non-equilibrium but also by processes of homeostasis which repeatedly re-new the threatened balance.

New Urban Design Parameters. In my opinion, it is from a systemic approach that we need to rediscover the concrete specificities of the urbanistic discipline to open possibilities for the complexity of the *Urban Turn Two*. In respect of this, here following I will introduce a series of urban design parameters - correlated to

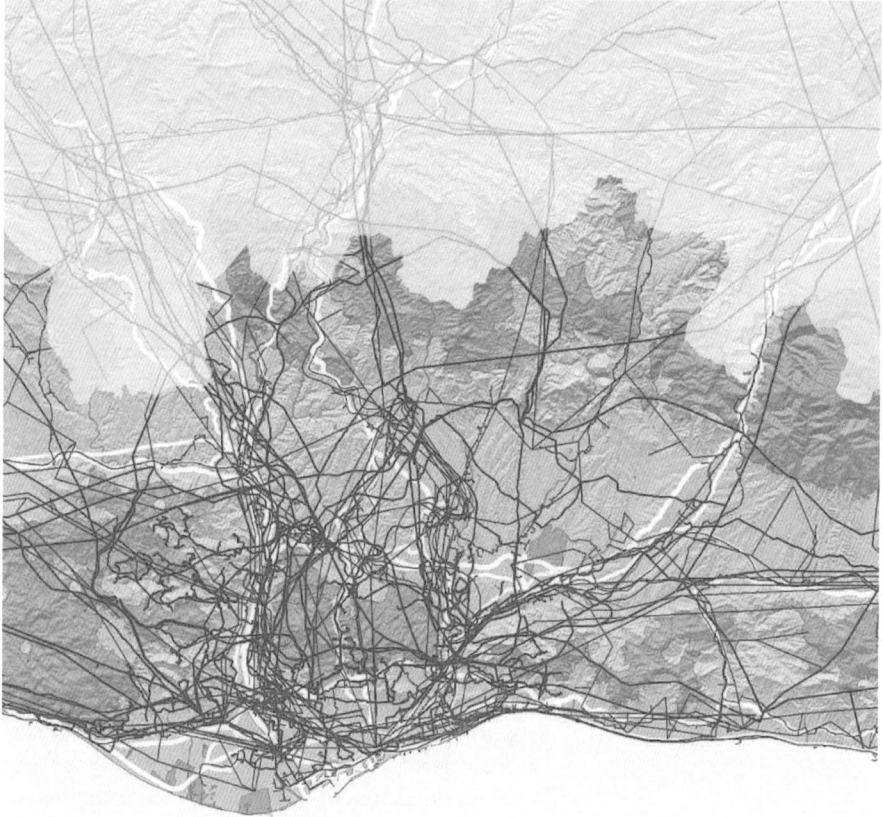

"Networks for Land": Barcelona's infrastructural network complexity.
courtesy of Barcelona Regional Metropolitan Agency

fig. 1

the slogan *Networks for Land* - which I have been experiencing in my work as an architect for the City of Barcelona over the last 30 years.

Isotropy. New infrastructures, since their immateriality, easily unfold on the territory and, on the contrary of the traditional ones, are apparently not selective in respect of its physical characteristics. Therefore, with new infrastructures, it is easier to develop and re-develop territories of any kind augmenting their capacity, even in the case of places once discarded because of their geographical un-accessibility. It could be even possible to say that nowadays "everything is possible everywhere", a statement clearly breaking the modern dogmas of ergonomy and stimulating the production of territories "a là carte".

Interstitiality. Contemporary infrastructural provisions are better distributed through capillary networks rather than through those centralized collectors which were characterizing the modern infrastructures. Capillary networks, through their interstitiality, essentially aim at increasing service accessibility. Moreover they supply other spatial services: while permitting to redeem and augment "intermediate urban spaces", once hidden or forgotten because of their accessibility, their interstitiality induces the differentiation of mobility systems and therefore introduces "attractiveness" in the realm of mobility. The incorporation of interstitiality within urban fabrics in fact increases their functional flexibility and their consequent capacity to permit random processes. From this perspective, constructing interstitiality is one of the most important duties of today's urban design: even if we are not in an historical moment in which a small program of boulevards, abruptly breaking up the pre-existing urban fabric as in Haussmann's Paris, is enough to completely change the city, it is precisely the project of accessibility in all of its interstitial graduations that is crucial for the definition of contemporary public space.

00 h 20 min

Fracmentation. In the light of the progressive urban complexity, nowadays it is simply administratively unsustainable to defend the notion of the city as a unitary organism, even if it is still politically necessary. In respect to this, conceptualizing the city as a networked system of several urban patches appears to be an interesting attempt at overcoming the paradoxes embedded in such notions of the city we are still operating with. Fracmentation is the parameter characterizing this appealing conceptualization: it essentially defines a relationship between the parts and the totality of a system in respect of their possibility of autonomy as well as of integration. In a way, since it highlights the systemic difference among a whole and its constitutive parts, an adequate level of fracmentation could spatially support both local identities and an overall sense of tolerance—a perfect framework for integration in the nowadays urban processes of socio-cultural complexification.

If the degree of heterogeneity and of parts variability determines the degree of complexity of a system, complexity appears in reality to essentially be the composite manifestation of a certain dimensionality and fracmentation. The crucial question to manage urban system therefore appears to be the establishment of what is the most convenient size for every spatial or temporal level of development. In respect to the implicit move towards the understanding of the city as a process of development that is contained in its systemic understanding, when we consider the actual necessity to project urban fracmentation, the design of joints among urban patches become as much important as the design of the patches in themselves: while offering cognitive reliability for the overall system, joints occupy space and time provisionally in order to maintain room for further development.

Icebergs. Between 5% and 10% of the Earth surface is occupied by caves formed by the dissolution of calcium carbonates, which can also be exploited for new programs. In respect of this capacity, the underground must be considered as a reservoir for the future, and must be re-evaluated according this opportunity. A new inter-relationship aboveground / underground already constitutes the base for a new metropolitan complexity and for augmenting the functional thickness of the territory: as in the icebergs, in contemporary buildings we can just appreciate that small amount which emerges from the ground surface, but not what stays submerged.

Even if underground space has always been a reference for human life, modernity has assigned to it only secondary functions, giving instead to the ground level the superior capacity of integrating green, housing and in general all the principal functions of modern life. By the way, the perception of the underground is today positively mutating for several reasons: underground doesn't provoke visual or acoustic impact on the territory; it facilitates safety; it is energy saving in terms of environmental control; its development has become technologically and economically feasible thanks to contemporary constructive techniques; and finally its imaginary has become less gloomy thanks to the new technologies.

For example, I. M. Pei's Louvre Pyramid precisely embodies this concept with 28,000 sqm of new commercial activities, which are absolutely necessary for the sustainability of the overall museum institution, literally buried underground. Only one element emerges: the glass pyramid which illuminates the underground lobby. When I talked about it with Pei, he concisely replied: "It would have been simply impossible to spatially resolve this enormous program aboveground". And, I would add, to create any other agreement between the various architectural and cultural sensibilities of the city of Paris would have been equally impossible.

Intermodality. In a certain way an essential characteristic of the contemporary condition is the increase of our personal mobility. A new nomadism defines our life, fostering a form of mobility the more and more random, which implies many distinct transportation systems interlinked in a manifold web for achieving a higher accessibility and efficiency. In this context, the intermodal centre is the place where all the distinct transportation systems encounter and intersect each other. An urban space, where such confluence of flows is given, is obviously characterized by the passage of a huge number of people and finally implies a higher urban activity and the status of urban centrality. The exploitation of intermodality as the base for defining urban centralities is a key to effectively remap the contemporary territory.

In my opinion, at the urban level, intermodal centres operate a metabolic regulatory role similar to the one performed by the liver for the entire human body. We have to understand intermodal centres not just as the crossing point of material and immaterial flows within the city, but really as centralities which operates in respect to the overall urban body.

Barcelona's La Sagrera station is the biggest project among European hubs of this kind and it will be completed within two or three years: high-speed lines, rail lines, metro lines, and a bus station are vertically arranged to improve the level of intermodality. It is forecast that 125 million people will transit through the station in the first year, a concentration obviously generating great human intensity and therefore clearly becoming an urban and regional centre.

Recycling. We should then review the concept of restoration: while it is clearly necessary to restore architectural masterpieces, it is also clear that we cannot continue with the aspiration to keep and maintain all the buildings from the past. In architecture, the recycling through the intervention in historical master-

Josep Acebillo

00 h 30 min

pieces architectures has always been a positive source of creativity and modernity (i.e. Vicenza's Basilica and Palladio, Rome's Santa Maria degli Angeli and Michelangelo, etc...). Now the question is: do we have to consider urban architecture as something absolutely permanent, which must be therefore the object of maintenance, or as something, passed its moment, to be recycled or substituted?

Gregotti warns us on the danger of a new architecture based on maintaining the old: it is instead needed to project, incorporating the idea of future-use. The urban space needs to live and renovate, accepting that destruction is in any case the base for any new step of development. In many cities, the functional variations of some of their parts, combined with the programmatic strengthening possible through reuse and recycling, open space to a crucial urban dynamism. For example in the contemporary city, especially in the post-industrial era, enormous spaces more or less obsolete are appearing, as the result of the processes of industrial delocalization. This situation is the source for new possibility of urban transformation involving the invention of new productive and urban types (i.e. Canary Wharf in London, Chelsea in New York, etc...). Barcelona's 22@ redevelopment—the most modern technological district we have in this moment in Barcelona—was clearly based on such premises: it was the biggest industrial district of the Cerdà Ensanche, which was no longer suitable for industrial purposes, and we have been carefully selecting which buildings are to be preserved and restored to their original forms, which are to be reused and therefore "dynamically" restored, and which are to be demolished in order to make way for new buildings. Thanks to this operation, 4 million sqm for new activities will be available in the near future, regenerating the neighbourhood life.

Interactivity. Another parameter is following the technological development which has made possible

New Urban Design Parameters at stake: Barcelona 1980-2010.
courtesy of Barcelona Regional Metropolitan Agency

fig. 2

Josep Acebillo

a constant reconfiguration of the interactions between urban users and their environment. Space and time have always been the objects of architecture, but those nowadays have been augmented by the appearance of an essentially interactive virtual space which mediate our relationship to the immediate environment. Interactive virtuality has gradually invaded our culture, and this asks for new thesis for architecture and urban development. In fact, the dynamic feedbacks possible in the interactive virtuality are opening a gap between the modern binomial *Form—Function* and asking for its substitution with a trinomial *Form—Flow—Function* still to be understood and unfolded. The Chicago Millennium Park is a very clear example: Chicago has almost no traditional public space because of its harsh climate. Frank O. Gehry, commissioned to build a big auditorium, has therefore refused to design another building but has preferred to create an open-air space with new technologies making it possible both to fulfil the required function and to keep the space publicness: a canopy with sound emitters numerically controlling sound has finally enriched a public space with an acoustic quality comparable to that of a concert hall. Another example is the Federal Plaza in Melbourne, one of the most "efficient" public spaces in the world thanks to the interaction made possible by technology: the entire complex is like an enormous TV studio with which people can interface while walking.

New Urban Theory Frameworks. In any case, the theoretical analysis of the new urban complexity contextualizes in respect of what I consider four interrelated frameworks: *Urban Intensity, Urbanity, Urban Metabolism,* and *Neometropolitanism.*
In respect of this, I must note that such fragmentation of the theoretical analysis is not contrary to a holistic vision of the city. The very question is in fact the visual-

ization of the actual polyedric character of the urban space rather than its actual unity: a holistic vision becomes more effective and responsive to reality only with the possibility of a transversal reading between different subsystems of analysis.

Urban components, in fact, can always be read from different perspective: we can for example understand the urban public space as the key point to promote a new urban cluster with high programmatical intensity; or we can understand the urban public space as a platform to solve the problems of coexistence and to promote intercultural cooperation; or we can understand the urban public space as a physical platform for the matter and energy fluxes that defines the metabolic efficiency of the city; or we can understand the urban public space as a "matrix" that structures interactions in the polycentric nature of the neometropolitan space. All of these approaches, which frameworks are following in a summary, are not alternative but rather complementary ones.

Urban Intensity. (☞"The city [as] a large, dense and permanent settlement of heterogeneous people", Louis Wirth). In a contemporary territorial perspective, the compact urban fabric must confront the sprawl urbanisation; consequently the key points to define this framework are: *Density Variability, Compactness & Porosity, Functional Hibridity.*

Urbanity. (☞"What is the city, but the people?", William Shakespeare). In the light of the urban global restructuring, the new socio-cultural approach should be characterized by: *General Accessibility to Urban Commons, Housing Affordability, Public Space Plurality, "Creative Milieux".*

Urban Metabolism. (☞"The city [as] an organism which requires nutrients and energy, stores and produces waste", Peter Newman). Understanding the city as a set of thermodynamic process characterized by the intermittence between dissipative and homeostatic

Josep Acebillo

tendencies, the key points to define this framework are: *Metabolism Circularity, New Postindustrial Mobility Matrix* (share of on-demand and discretional transport), *"Urban Action but Slim City", Urban Resilience.*

Neometropolitanism. (☞ "Networks for Land"). If in opposition to industrial metropolitanism, where land values were displaced according geographical conditions, a neometropolitanism in which the city-region is the true horizon must consider the characteristics of existing and potential networks too as the basis for the analysis of the territory and its design, the key points to define this framework are: *"Ecologic Mosaic", Metropolitan Corridors Efficiency, Metropolitan Clusterization, Archipelago model based on a differentiated and hierarchic urban polycentrism.*

3.
Glocal Interactions in the Globalization of Urbanity. After

having framed the emergent urban question in the light of a progressive complexity, I will finally analyze the issue of globalization.

This, besides being of general relevance since it is swallowing the lives of everyone of us, is relevant from a territorial disciplinary perspective since it is crucially affecting the space / time relationship as well as the dialectic between homogeneity and heterogeneity, key variants of any territorial model.

Following Zygmunt Bauman, here we will briefly analyze the globalized condition in respect of its connections with the territorial culture, to ultimately end up in a complex and novel concept, the *Glocal*, which embodies an optimized interaction between the *Global* and the *Local* while potentially offering itself as a possible territorial thesis to come.

The process of national states power reduction we witness today is not an occasional phenomenon but something premeditated by the main actors of globalization. The sudden collapse of the block-politics, which took place in the nineties with the fall of the USSR, clarified that in the New World things were actually not controlled as before. Since then "the world is no longer perceived as a whole, but as a field of scattered and uneven forces that crystallize in very different places sometimes difficult to foresee, and that offer impulses that no one knows how to control". The idea of universalization in force since the World War implied a *New World Order* which, even if it was promoting different models of society according to the reference politic block, brought hope for development. But, after the collapse of the block-politics, the idea of universalization has been abruptly replaced by the idea of "globalization, which expresses the indeterminate, unruly and self-propelled nature characterizing global governance". Somehow, the new globalization thesis exemplified what Kenneth Jowitt defined as the *New World Disorder*. This evolution, by many considered an involution of global governance, has been very significant in many respects. For those interested in the urbanistic discipline, it is particularly relevant the way in which the new condition of globalization affected both the culture and the territorial thesis, a manifold operating from different perspectives and with different weapons. The prominence of this territorial discourse now dilutes without interruption, undoubtedly resulting from the diffusion of new technologies—essentially intangible and with no physical mass—which leads to lower spatial impact deployment and which creates a condition of isotropy equalizing the functional capacities of different kinds of territory. Some authors, such as Paul Virilio or Richard O. Brien, already in the nineties advanced the "end of geography", as a forecast of what globalization would have meant for the territorial culture. In fact, the high speed driven by new technology today defines an "acceleration" permeating our lives and subverting traditional notions of "proximity and distance". When Marc Augé says that contemporary life is characterized by three excesses—that is of time, space and individuality—he wants to highlight what this contemporary acceleration is actually implying for our lives and for their territorial context: "the distance is no longer an objective concept, and becomes a social product" since its extension, ceasing to be fixed, turns to be dependent on the speed that we can take in the socio-economical sphere of activity.

The emergent modality of the relation space / time, resulting from the technological revolution and possible thanks to the processes of globalization, has therefore a crucial territorial corollary: the "dissolution"—or "porosity"—of borders, which more and more blur, fade away, or suddenly re-appear. So present in our lives and so crucial for architecture and urban planning, the conventional notions of "here and there", "near and far", "inside or outside", finally occupy a much more relative and politicized territory. In fact, in the meanwhile Bill Clinton can say "no longer exists a difference between the internal or external policy", we can witness the worldwide appearance of constructed urban boundaries to cause social discrimination or even of second-class citizens groups so much obsessed with safety to adopt a voluntary form of urban segregation.

In any case, beyond the impact that new technologies and infrastructure are implying in the territorial culture of the globalized age, it is very possible to feel the tendency towards "deterritorialization" in the progressive limitations and even operative extinction of the modern concept of national State. The discourse of universalization was absolutely consistent with an idea of State explicitly assigned to a particular territory: the modern State has born tied to a specific territorial vision. For example, the birth of Canada has been generated by three particular actions: the drafting and

00 h 50 min

enactment of a territorialized Constitution; the adoption of a regulatory law limiting trade between Canada and the US; and finally the construction of a coast to coast railroad that would have given measure to Canada vastness.

On the contrary, globalization challenges the State because it does not require the territorial support for its deployment. When Max Weber defined the State "as the entity that claims the monopoly of the means of coercion within its sovereign territory", he clearly pointed out the territoriality embedded in the modern concept of State, whose sovereignty resides on military economic and cultural autonomy. In this sense, it is curious and at the same time sad to think how the possibility of a European state sovereignty could really be sustained while being based on the tripod of autonomy that we have just stated.

The concept of borders, today blurred by new technologies, appeared in fact as a result of the territoriality inherent in the concept of the State. The State needed "clear boundaries" that define its sovereignty, and if necessary they would have been strongly defended, something which clearly contrasts with the border porosity resulting from the globalization process.

It must be in fact noted that this dissolution of boundaries is often complemented by a strong structural randomness. In the European Union in fact we perceive both the porosity of the internal borders between the EU countries and the strength and intransigence of some EU edges areas aiming to avoid unwelcomed migration from the Far East or Africa. And in the same time, it is also increasingly frequent the occurrence of boundaries internal to our cities designed with the aim to "esclusiv-ize" concrete urban spaces, although this is due both to the negative obsession with security and privatization, that is typical of the globalized society, and to a positive administrative approach—in which the urban landscape is considered a mosaic—that considers the holistic functioning of the city not oppositional but consistent with its fragmented appearance.

Apparently the weakening of the modern State and the rise of new "anonymous power" do their best to "release the brakes of governance": deregulation, liberalization, relaxation, relief of tax burden, etc... in fact look to undermine state powers. But precisely at this point an interesting dialectic appears. Are we sure that global powers are really interested in weak States, unable to control territory, in order to replace them with global entities? In fact it is not. The State should be dismantled only up to certain limits, and in any case sometime instead of sharpening contradictions it appears better to create systems of cooperation. Only in this sense, "the political fragmentation and economic globalization are close allies".

But here, where the "cohabitation" starts to impose itself as a necessity, we get a question by the democratic institutions: who is the better prepared to assume responsibility for managing the territory? Probably the answer is not as objective as it should because our history and ideological baggage are very personal, but I still consider a majority would answer adopting a "subsidiary principle"—which means major territorial problems can be better resolved at lower levels than at upper ones—which frame Local Authorities, or the City and particularly Metropolitan Areas, as the best places to safeguard territorial coherence and efficiency.

Several reasons support this idea but essentially the fact that here we're not talking about "huge generic territories", that might be relevant as reserves for geostrategic and military reasons, but about "specific urban areas", in which industrial and tertiary production concretely take place.

In the light of this, the statistic projections give us a

	Industrial context	Glocal context
Governance	National States	Supranational Organizations
Economy	Fordist Production	Postfordist Networked Production
Technology	Heavy Infrastructures	Disruptive Infrastructures
Urban Intensity	Low Density & Sprawl	High Density & Compactness
Urban Character	Urban Icons	Slim Cities
Urbanity	Public Space Scarcity & Social Facilities	Public Space Plurality & Creative Commons
Housing Model	Social Housing	Affordable Housing
Urban Metabolism	Linear Metabolism	Circular Metabolism
Urban Critical Mass	Mega Cities & Business Efficiency	Midsize Cities & Ecological Efficiency*
Metropolitanism	Expansion vs. Concentration	Policentrism & Clusterization (City Region)
Mobility Matrix	Collective Transport	Personal & On-demand Transport
Design methodology	Plans	Projects & Strategic thinking

* Ecological efficiency operates both in economical and environmental terms.

Urban paradigm evolution: from the Industrial to the post-crisis Glocal context.
courtesy of Josep Acebillo

fig. 3

very clear insight: if demographically speaking our world will move from 7,000 billion to 9,000 billion people from 2010 to 2040, this huge population will essentially be living in cities—between 70% and 90%—occupying less than 3% of the planet ground. We are actually witnessing a globalization of urbanity unknown so far by both its size and complexity.

If therefore these data are revealing how our global future will be more and more connected to urban development, we cannot disagree with the fact that "the city will gradually assume a greater protagonism, and therefore global policies should not be dissociated with respect to local politics".

This new process of "recovery of the local as a counterweight to the global", essentially advertised and defended by those which professional background has a certain municipal spirit, is gradually strengthening around the world—obviously according to the local specificities—and it is already being addressed by some theorists, among which Donald Robertson that sees in glocali-zation, as a constant interaction between global and local, "the indissoluble unity of the globalizing and localizing pressures which generate not only capital and resources accumulation but also an increase in their capacity to be mobilized". In this sense *Glocal* refers to persons and institutions able to "think globally and act locally" and if in economic terms it means that "global companies should be adapted to the peculiarities of each envi-ronment, differentiating their products according to local demands", and if at cultural level it means that "in a world where borders are removed, filters will be appearing to defend cultural identity and traditions", at the disciplinary level it could mean an opportunity for architecture and urban planning, till today almost irrelevant in the deterritorialised condition of global processes, to acquire relevance in a *Glocal* urban future today marked by uncertainty.

intermezzo

Aleksandar Ivancic, mechanical engineer with a PhD in Thermal Science, works for Barcelona Regional, the Metropolitan Agency for Urban Development and Infrastructures. The main area of his professional interest is in infrastructure planning, with a particular focus on energy systems. In 2002-2003 he was Technical Director of the Barcelona Energy Agency and is presently Chief Technical Officer of Barcelona Strategic Urban Systems and Professor at the BiArch—Barcelona Institute of Architecture. He has published more than fifty scientific and technical papers in journals and books, relating to urban infrastructures, renewable energies, renewable integration in urban space, energy planning, heat and mass transfer and computational fluid dynamics. Recently, Gustavo Gili published his book "Energyscapes".

Energyscapes: on territory and energy.

I should like to thank the organizers and Professor
Acebillo for having invited me to join you today.
I will talk about energy in the urban environment as
well as in our wider environment, giving some insight
into an energy world which is full of contradictions
and full of strange things that are difficult to realize
in conceptual terms. I invite you to reflect upon the
aberration of the territorial isotropy that Professor
Acebillo has just presented: when you go skiing in
the Emirates this implies an intensive form of energy
consumption, nothing but energy transformation, or a
process which generates entropy. Through what is,
in my opinion, our still old-fashioned "world vision",
we are generating tremendous entropy which makes
our energy paradigm quite simply inappropriate. The
energy paradigm shift is one of the most challenging
problems facing our society at the beginning of
the twenty-first century and I think this is not just a

technological challenge, but a social and intellectual challenge too: we need to consider how to change the behavior of all of us, as citizens, professionals and politicians as well.

Energy paradigm shift paradoxes. Energy is closely related to development and political freedom, as UN indicators show: more energy consumed corresponds to more human development, and more energy corresponds to greater political freedom. But is this sustainable? Can we really rely on the trends these figures suggest? Actually, since energy is connected to carbon emissions, it is also possible to consider from a different perspective the implications of human development and political freedom and wealth in general… In the light of this, what is ultimately happening today? Are we actually de-carbonizing our world? The reply is yes, our energy production systems are emitting less and less carbon, but their efficiency is still far from the ratio of energy / carbon emission that would prevent global warming. Unfortunately, we still have to tackle big problems to reach that ratio. From another point of view, energy consumption and energy demand must be linked to population growth simply because it is true that while our per capita use of energy is rising, we are also becoming more numerous. In respect of this, the only apparent way to stabilize human population levels, according to demography experts, would be to eradicate poverty. But eradicating poverty essentially means encouraging some 5 billion people to consume more energy, as the previous considerations suggest, thus magnifying the contradictions of energy paradigm shifts. Today, every week cities like Barcelona consume the energy that was needed to construct the great Cheops pyramid in Giza. I think this gives a good idea of our present consumption trend. And keep in mind that Barcelona is a fairly efficient city. In respect of this, we can also consider gross values and development scenarios: the Swiss concept of the "2000-Watt society"—an amount which corresponds to a fair share of the per-capita capacity of the biosphere which we can assume an ecological world could be based on—implies that we should reduce our consumption to approximately a third of the current European average. Or a sixth of the US average. You can imagine what a huge effort we need to make to reduce our consumption to such an extent.

And if we are not able to so, what will happen? I hope you have read the recent book called *Collapse* by the Pulitzer-prize-winner Jared Diamond: it talks about what happens in an isolated society in which consumption exceeds available resources... I do not want to be a pessimist but it is clear we need new ideas and a lot of hard work on these issues.

Energy and the city. As I have just said, the global population is growing and the world is also becoming more and more urbanized, which means that urban space is central to the sustainability issue of our future. Without doubt, the main improvements and changes will have to take place in our cities both technologically and in terms of our citizens' behavior. If we review history, the shape and form of cities have always been related to the availability of energy: looking at our historic cities, it is extremely rare to find more than half million inhabitants when they are based on traditional energy systems, and biomass and wind in particular. But then, with the increase of energy made available by fossil sources, cities changed shape completely: on one hand they started to grow in terms of surface area, expanding beyond their former walls and spreading out like an oil slick, while on the other they started to grow vertically with buildings growing taller. In a way, while the very flat shape of the medieval city turned to a bell shape

01 h 10 min

along with what Professor Acebillo calls the industrial Urban Turn, I think it is very relevant to wonder what urban shapes will be like in the twenty-first century. Or more precisely, are energy limitations and scarcity going to determine the shape and pattern of urban growth in the near future? Beyond the obvious relevance of this, I consider the subject crucial with regard to the question of optimum city size, and therefore to the very reasons for an archipelago-style urban model.

A possible pathway for answering such questions would be to argue about the integration of energy systems in our lives, or rather the integration of our lives in energy systems and in those necessary artifacts which support our life. Gunkajima island in Japan offers a very interesting example to inspire contemporary urban projects like Norman Foster's Masdar city. This small island was the headquarters of a company town for a community of workers operating in the coal mines placed under the sea level of the same island territory. Probably, this was the most densely populated city in the world history—1,400 people per hectare, which means 10 times the density of Barcelona today and 100 times the density of Lugano—and energy was its most important systemic symbol.

Behind energy consumption. Here I would like to stress how much some of the most significant factors which lead to energy consumption have grown in today's cities. The Heat Island Effect, Generic Architecture, the demand for comfort, electronic equipment, and overfeeding are some of the decisive factors of this problem.

Urban Heat island. This, for example, is a phenomenon well known by specialists but often ignored by general professionals. It literally corresponds to the generation of a "heat bubble"

Aleksandar Ivancic

which is hard to dissipate in the wider environment and it depends on the materials we are using to cover urban surfaces. More precisely, it depends to a large extent on their optical characteristics and permeability. This is because of the crucial link between the territorial balance of energy and the natural water cycle, heat, and the possibility of mass transfer. We can easily see differences in ambient temperatures of between 5 and 10 °C due just to surface changes from impervious to water to vegetal matter. The atmospheric water which reaches the land surface is part of an important mechanism through which heat is released and dissipated by evaporation, and this process is possible only in the presence of water. If there is no water, evaporation cannot take place, nor can heat dissipation. Thus, one of the most important factors in the relationship with heat islands and their eventual control is actually related to the way in which we treat the water cycle, a concept strictly tied to infrastructures, pavements and the management of rain water.

Generic architecture. One problem the world of architects is used to is an excess of generic architecture: out of place, more or less subjected to overabundant iconic demand, responsive neither to the climate nor to the context. In the midst of the contemporary crisis, this kind of architecture is, I think, absolutely finished and condemned to be replaced by greater attention to traditional wisdom and responsive environmental considerations.

Demand for comfort. A crucial issue is to be found in the definition of the demand for comfort: the notion of comfort has changed tremendously in recent years; for example in Britain the average temperature in inhabited spaces rose from the 13 °C in the '70s to 19 °C today, a difference of 6 °C, obviously implying higher energy consumption. In any case I have to clarify that I'm not stating that 13 °C is more appropriate but simply that we are progressively consuming more energy. And in the same period, for example in the States, the average residential area per person has grown by 50%, exponentially multiplying the implications of the previous evidence.

Electronic equipment. Electronic equipment is becoming progressively important in our built environment, making the heat dissipation it involves that much more relevant: all computer functions, and everything that requires electrons to move, even on the nano scale, heats up its surrounding space.

Overfeeding. Finally I want to touch on the fact that we are overfeeding ourselves, ingesting excessive calories, in reality well beyond what is necessary. As a consequence of this, even in places where the demand for refrigeration would not normally be considered, cooling must be introduced to respond to the metabolic effects of our overfeeding. And you can imagine what this means for Mediterranean, sub tropical or tropical cities...

Another set of problems, related to urban infrastructures, could include personal mobility systems, "use once and throw away" habits, unoptimized infrastructure networks, nutrient flux management, low power-density renewables.

Personal mobility systems. In terms of future development, I think mobility is one of the crucial problems in terms of its growing unsustainability. However, people are going to move more and more. If we accept this, there is in any case a contradiction in personal mobility systems which have progressively tended to rely on bigger and bigger vehicles with lower and lower occupancy. I was personally surprised to see the admiration for vehicles like the Hummer—a famous and now widely used SUV—conceived as a military vehicle and not an urban car, even though some of us are using it as a vehicle for personal mobility. I'm afraid this tendency will spread to the entire urbanized world...

01 h 30 min

Aleksandar Ivancic

"Use once and throw away" habits. The culture of disposable products is also generating a tremendous quantity of waste and is thus also creating another challenge to be faced in respect to the issues of reuse and recycling of all kinds.

Unoptimized infrastructure networks. Another problem is our unoptimized infrastructure network. Talking about the service infrastructures of energy, water, and waste, I think we have to learn to tackle them together in order to search for synergies and to optimize the functionalities of our urban systems. Industrial ecology concepts should therefore demand a big step forward in our attempt to transform our way of operating large technical systems and to consider how the urban fabric and city life constitute productive processes can be reined in. Here metabolic and life-cycle analysis is absolutely crucial.

Nutrient flux management. Energy, waste and water networks directly relate to the question of nutrient fluxes. Natural environment systems usually reuse all kinds of materials, not excluding waste, which actually becomes a resource for subsystems which reintroduce its constituents into the system's metabolic cycle. Regarding nutrient flux, today we tend to ignore it, and we are actually "throwing away" nutrients which are still useful and in theory recoverable. To move beyond this pointless approach, we need to question how such quickly discarded nutrients are often released into rivers and seas, or generally into the water system: while this implies a dangerous erosion of nutrients from the land, threatening agricultural production, the passage of these nutrients into water is provoking eutrophication, negatively affecting the aquatic environment. This is related to energy due to the potential for organic waste digestion and for the production of both methane and compost. Besides using methane for energy purposes, natural soil fertilization reduces the demand for the energy-consuming manufacture of artificial fertilizers.

Low power-density renewables. The interesting but commonly misunderstood problem of renewables addresses their very low power density: through renewable energy harvesting we can extract limited amounts of energy in large extensions of space, with the consequent need for a tremendous amount of space to collect a significant quantity of energy required by our contemporary society. Unfortunately we still have environmental gurus who claim we can easily pass to renewables and we also have politicians without any real knowledge of them: a terrible risk. We need renewables but we need to be very careful about the real potential of each of them,

and what they can reasonably be expected to provide us. To illustrate this briefly, I would like to remind you about how some years ago the European Commission promoted a policy fostering the production of biomass. However, to reach the potential estimated by the EC—less than 9% of EU energy demand—a territory larger than the whole of the Czech Republic, Estonia and Hungary combined would be needed. To be quite clear, this means that we would need much more land for bio energy production than what we have available. On the other hand, we can easily realize how the devices we are using now for renewable energy production are tremendously big. Considering the most recent technologies, we are talking about 250-meter-tall wind turbines or dozens of hectares under a single solar power plant, and these are sizes which tend to increase. We have huge installations as well as massive territory-consuming practices for the production of limited quantities of electricity...

A new integration of the energy system into our lives.

Why am I explaining this? I'm explaining this in order to clarify my position with regard to the issue of renewables, which clearly demands a new form

Aleksandar Ivancic

of integration in the city. I usually refer to a pyramid diagram in order to clarify my approach on the subject of renewables: at the base, there must be a reduction in demand, which implies everything I've mentioned so far, from heat island mitigation to the use of intelligent systems, passive architecture, etc… Then, on the second level, the question of transformation and end-use efficiency: end-use efficiency requires comprehensive efficiency of all the machines we have in our built environment to make it work, and as well as those related specifically to infrastructures and urban services. Later on, one should think about the recovery and reuse of waste energy, in so-called cascading processes. Finally, once all these steps have been accomplished, the turn comes to harvest renewables. Only like this, by first reducing demand and optimizing processes, renewables can constitute a significant portion of our supply.

Coming back to process optimization, we also need to reflect on low-tech and high-tech devices. We are often seduced by new technologies but we also need to take care of technologies and concepts that have often been used down the centuries. Especially in climatic terms. Addressing the specifics of high tech, we need to make a distinction between standard solutions and tailor-made ones, which can perform extremely well but with a level of value for money that is often less interesting than that of major available solutions, obviously cheaper. As an example of such question, I would like to highlight the Swedish case of snow used for cooling, which combines contemporary technology with a traditional technique that was used even before cooling machines were invented around 150 years ago: in ancient times the people used to preserve snow throughout the seasons, storing it and keeping it in special conditions in order to make use of it throughout the year. A hospital in Sweden uses a very simple method of snow-cooling, managing an area of snow landfill and then insulating it with a half-meter layer of forest wood-chip waste which prevents the snow from melting and means it can be used for cooling throughout the year. Other similar techniques are possible, for district cooling, or generically centralized cooling systems are used in Paris, Stockholm and Toronto, which use their river, sea or lake water for direct cooling. Another possibility is sky radiation. A very interesting mechanism for cooling the Earth is simply a clear night sky: the intriguing heat effect that occurs in deserts, where extremely high day temperatures coincide with extremely low temperatures at night, largely depends on the fact that the clear sky, without humidity and cloud, permits rapid heat dissipation by radiation. This can be used also in buildings in climates where the absence of clouds makes it possible to take advantage of this radiative cooling mechanism. On the subject of high tech, a lot of things are already available: just think about new super-insulation, transparent insulation or photovoltaic materials, electric vehicles, smart power grids and other intelligent systems... We are now also witnessing a huge effort in the production of non-standard forms and fabrics or textiles with inserted PV energy collection systems. Tailor-made solutions are sometimes very fancy—i.e. like wind generators in skyscrapers— and can be implemented paradigmatically. But we can also talk about less glamorous things: in Barcelona, for example, we have a tailor-made installation which reuses waste coolness coming from the industrial plants in the harbour, which use liquid natural gas conversion after its transportation. Natural gas travels in a liquid state, where it is maintained at 150°C degrees below zero, and it is necessary to heat it up in order to evaporate it before injecting it into the gas network. The installations which perform this operation normally use sea water as their heat source. We have been promoting the recovery of this cooling energy and it can be used to air-condition the district through a proper network. These systems have tremendous potential but I think this approach needs tailor-made solutions in order to reach its technical potential, which in the case mentioned may signify a 10% reduction of total electricity consumption in Barcelona. This really deserves special attention. In Barcelona too, on the other side of the city, there are also less tailor-made solutions, with more standard examples of heat recovery from urban solid waste treatment that is used for district heating and cooling. Finally, I would mention that besides the question of energy systems, energy artifacts of the recent past are very interesting in terms of urbanity and in terms of the re-development of urban spaces. As you may have noticed, there is a trend to convert power plants and other industrial relics which, for functional reasons, were once at the edge of the city, and often on the waterfront. But now, many of them have become technologically obsolete and, as a consequence of city growth, surrounded by the urban realm. After disuse, they offer opportunities for creating new urban centralities that would be impracticable elsewhere. This is partly because today's technology improvements make it possible to build smaller energy infrastructures, reducing the spatial need for technical installations, but also reducing protection zones thanks to cleaner technologies. Ultimately, these entail the emergence of new empty spaces which are suitable for reinventing the city. In this sense, Barcelona's Forum 2004 is a clear example of where a technological upgrading of power generation plants has permitted their integration in a new urban space and the creation of a new public area with complex diversity.

Christian Schmid, was born in Zurich in 1958 and studied Geography and Sociology at the University of Zurich. Since 1982, he has been active as an urban researcher and as an organizer of cultural events. He was part of the group SAU—Ssenter for Applied Urbanism, and worked in the Rote Fabrik cultural centre. He has authored, co-authored, and co-edited numerous publications on Zurich's urban development, on urban and regional planning and international comparative analysis, and on theories of the city and of space. In 1991, he was a cofounder of the INURA—International Network for Urban Research and Action. In 1993-94, he was a fellow researcher at the Laboratoire de Géographie Urbaine, Université Paris X Nanterre, and in 1995-96 he worked in the interdisciplinary research project "La ville: villes de crise ou crise des villes", Institut d'Architecture, Université de Genève. From 1997-2001 he was an assistant lecturer at the Geography Department of the University of Bern. In 1999, he became the scientific director of the "Switzerland—An Urban Portrait" project at ETH Studio Basel. A book with the same title was published in 2005, authored by Roger Diener, Jacques Herzog, Marcel Meili, Pierre de Meuron and Christian Schmid. Since 2001, he has been a lecturer in Sociology at the Faculty of Architecture of ETH Zurich. In 2003, he received his PhD from the Friedrich Schiller University in Jena. The book with the title "Stadt, Raum und Gesellschaft—Henri Lefebvre und die Theorie der Produktion des Raumes" was published in 2005. Since 2009 he has been Professor at the Faculty of Architecture of ETH Zurich.

Patterns and pathways of global urbanisation: towards comparative analysis.

The past two decades have seen a fundamental change in the speed, scale and scope of urbanisation. Transcending all forms of physical, political and social borders, urbanisation has become a global phenomenon. At the same time, differences both between and within cities have become more pronounced: despite the global sprawl of urban areas, the individual development of cities reveals considerable specificity and path dependency. This has led to the evolution of a wide range of different urban forms and constellations.

We are now faced with an urban universe that is constantly bringing forth new developments. The challenge is to improve our understanding of contemporary urbanisation processes and to analyse them, and establish their implications and effects. New concepts and terms are needed to designate these new urban forms and processes. Despite intense efforts, the concepts developed so far are not sufficient to describe and explain these new urban developments comprehensively. Little is yet understood about the form, extent, and implications of these urbanisation processes and their variations as they appear in different places. What is still lacking is a comparative approach enabling the detection and explanation of the differences that are developing today. The challenge is to further develop a comparative approach that is able to apprehend the general tendencies of urbanisation and at the same time to address the specificities of each urban area.

Tracing global urbanisation. Urban development has radically changed in recent years. All over the world, new patterns of urbanisation are evolving, "creating the most economically, socially, and culturally heterogeneous cities the world has ever known" (Soja and Kanai 2007). Existing urban forms are dissolving and polymorphous urban regions are taking shape. Extremely heterogeneous in structure, they include old city centres as well as formerly peripheral areas. At the same time, extremely rapid urbanisation has led to the emergence of completely new urban forms in the mega-cities of the global South: informal modes of urbanisation, which were long regarded as temporary aberrations, are increasingly becoming core elements of urban expansion that can no longer be ignored. It is instead to be expected that informal forms of urbanism will become a permanent feature of urban development.

Contemporary urbanisation is closely linked with globalization: in an increasingly networked world, industrialisation on a global scale has experienced massive acceleration and expansion. This has a dual effect on urbanisation: on the one hand, the new global economy has led to strong economic growth in cities, attracting a large number of migrants. Some cities have become centres of decision-making and innovation, and are developing into strategic nodes of the globalised economy (Sassen 1991, Scott 2000). Other cities, predominantly located in emerging economies, are attracting the growing global manufacturing industry. On the other hand, industrialisation and rationalisation of agriculture works as a push factor and causes additional migration from rural areas to the cities. The increasingly complex mechanisms of urban growth are further aggravated by continuing population growth in many parts of the world. Accelerated urbanisation leads to considerable concentration processes in already densely populated urban areas on the one hand, and to dramatic urban sprawl on the other, causing urban areas to massively expand towards the countryside (Angel et al. 2005, Lang 2003). In this way, globalization leads to an intensification of urbanisation, while urbanisation simultaneously acts as a major driving force of globalization. The unprecedented dimension and speed of urbanisation has dramatic consequences: today, there are around 500 city regions with populations exceeding 1 million, around 20 mega-city regions with over 10 million residents, and some extended urban areas, such as Tokyo and the Pearl River Delta, with more than 40 million inhabitants (Florida et al. 2008). These regions form large networked and strongly urbanised spaces, which are structured quite heterogeneously. They may include various agglomerations, metropolitan regions, and networks of cities, but also large green spaces and sparsely settled zones (Diener et al. 2005). Other far-reaching socio-spatial transformations include the blurring and re-articulation of urban territories, the disintegration of the "hinterland" and the end of the "wilderness" (Brenner and Schmid 2012).

Case studies and urban models. Until recently, urban research still remained largely dominated by monographs and analyses of individual cities. Accordingly, the understanding of urban development is to a large extent still determined by ideal-type models. As early as the 1920s, the Chicago School of Sociology used the example of Chicago as the basis for its famous concentric ring model of urban development (Park et al. 1925). In the 1990s, the Los Angeles School emerged as an antithetical model shaped largely by urban geography. It declared Los Angeles, which is characterised by urban sprawl and polycentricity, to be a paradigmatic example of urban development at the end of the twentieth century (Scott and Soja 1996). In architecture too, the emphasis was on learning from individual cities; well-known examples include *Learning from Las Vegas* (Venturi et al. 1972) and *Delirious New York* (Koolhaas 1978). These examples show that until the end of the twentieth century, the focus was mainly on developments in the West, especially in North America. This dominance of Western models has been increasingly questioned in recent times (Davis 2005, Roy 2008). Currently, there is a constant flow of new research and investigations of cities across the world. However, the overwhelming majority of these case studies continue to be monographs, leading again to the promotion of particular cities, such as Mexico City, Shanghai, Dubai, and Lagos as spectacular new examples of urban development. While such specific cases can be helpful for identifying typical new developments, they neither offer an overview, nor do they facilitate a differentiated analysis of urbanisation processes. Instead, there is a danger of generalisation based on spectacular individual cases or a reductionist view of highly complex, varied and differentiated processes that result in simplified models.

Christian Schmid

New processes of urbanisation. Another strand of urban research is the analysis of processes and phenomena. This focuses not so much on the individual city as on the process of urbanisation itself. This approach has gained prominence since the 1980s, when fundamental changes in urbanisation became visible and the attention shifted to entirely new aspects and processes, heralding a new phase of urban research and giving rise to new approaches and concepts. Many new concepts and terms have been developed in recent years to designate various new emerging urban phenomena (Taylor and Lang 2004). First, the emergence of global cities and world cities as strategic hubs of the global economy was investigated and the implications for urban development were studied (Friedmann 1986; Sassen 1991; Brenner and Keil 2006). Second, in a related field, the restructuring and upgrading of urban areas was analysed, with special attention given to processes such as gentrification and urban regeneration (Brenner and Theodore 2002, Smith 2002, Moulaert et al. 2003, Porter and Shaw 2009). Third, entirely new developments were observed in the suburban parts of metropolitan regions: here, a wide variety of new urban configurations and forms emerged and were referred to, among other names, as "edge cities" (Garreau 1991), "exopolis" (Soja 1992), and "Zwischenstadt" ("in-between cities", Sieverts 2003).

During the past decade, new tendencies have been detected. In particular, there has been the massive growth of cities in the global South and a trend towards mega-cities (Gugler 1997, Marcuse and van Kempen 2000), as well as the phenomenon of shrinking cities (Oswalt et al. 2006). Additionally, multiple forms of informal settlements and slums have emerged to an extent not previously known (Davis 2006, Neuwirth 2005, Roy and Al Sayyad 2004, Brillembourg et al. 2005).

The many anthologies and readers on these issues have led to important insights and given rise to interesting and important collections showing diverse examples of various aspects of global urbanisation. Many of these studies make use of a comparative perspective. Nevertheless, they usually remain as compilations of interesting case studies, bringing together the works of different authors. Accordingly, the examples are hardly comparable, and are not being subjected to systematic comparison. Furthermore, they usually remain focused on a single topic, which makes it difficult to get a comprehensive overview of current urbanisation processes.

On comparative urban studies. Demands for systematic comparative research in urban studies have been increasingly put forward (Nijman 2007, Ward 2008), and an ever-growing number of comprehensive analyses on individual aspects of global urbanisation have been published in recent years. Current examples include the *Multiplicity* project (Boeri et al. 2000), the studies conducted by the *Globalization and World Cities* research network (Taylor 2004), the INURA book on contested metropolises (INURA and Palosicia 2004), and a comparative study on European megacity regions (Hall and Pain 2006). Recently, some important surveys across the entire range of aspects of global urbanisation have been published. In particular, these include the catalogue of the Venice Biennale (Burdett and Ichioka 2006), *The Endless City*, part of the LSE's *Urban Age* project (Burdett and Sudjic 2007), and the geography of globalization (Lévy et al. 2008).

None of these examples, however, are comparative studies in the strictest sense. Efforts to carry out a comprehensive and systematic comparison of the urban development of cities are still in their early stages. One of the first systematic studies in this field is the detailed comparison of the historical development of the three US metropolises New York, Los Angeles, and Chicago by Abu-Lughod (1999). But major theoretical and methodical difficulties have arisen here too, and the result is more a parallel interpretation of the urban development of the three cities than a full comparative analysis (Brenner 2001). Simone (2004) offers further important input for comparative urban research and potential methodological advances in his comparison of four African cities, and Robinson (2006) introduces the remarkable proposal of analysing southern cities, which have hitherto been regarded as exotic, in a way that treats them as ordinary cities. Further efforts in comparative studies can be found e.g. in Boudreau et al. (2007), Kantor (2008), as well as in Wu and Phelps (2008).

As all these examples show, the comparative analysis of cities and urban areas is facing many difficulties. The complex processes involved in restructuring cities and urban regions require a new understanding of contemporary urbanisation. What is needed is a dynamic approach in urban studies that not only detects and describes the emergence of new urban forms but also focuses on the mechanisms of urbanisation processes and explains how general tendencies take shape in specific places. I shall now illustrate some of my own experiences in this field.

Capitales Fatales. The first comparative study I was involved in was an analysis of contemporary urban politics and the unfolding of new urbanisation processes in Zurich and Frankfurt (Hitz et al. 1995). This study was based on the theories on world cities and global cities that had just been introduced into German-speaking debate at that time. The two cities were analyzed by two separate teams in a parallel fashion, with the same basic concepts and analytical tools. It could

02 h 20 min

be seen that both cities are undergoing very similar processes: both are old industrial cities that have undergone massive economic restructuring in recent years, thus turning into global financial centres, and showing developments comparable to those of large global cities like New York or London. This is why we called them "capitales fatales". By focusing on the parallels of urban development in the two cities, it was possible to understand how globalization was produced and to identify the decisive elements of the urban transformation processes that reshape globalising cities: on the one hand, processes of urban restructuring and gentrification in the inner city areas were taking place, and on the other, the processes of restructuring the urban periphery were similar to those observed in North America at the same time. These developments also led to the emergence of a regional scale of urbanisation and opened up the question of new regional politics. At the same time, the effects of local politics and the strong influence of urban social movements on the urbanisation process were observed in both cities, thus indicating the strong articulation of global and local processes, a phenomenon which was conceptualised at the time by the term "glocalization" (Swyngedouw 1997).

The New Metropolitan Mainstream. Another example for such a comparative approach is the ongoing project of the INURA—International Network for Urban Research and Action on the "new metropolitan mainstream". This term has been coined to describe a broad range of phenomena that have recently emerged in cities around the world (Schmid 2011). Initially, this mainstream is articulated as a norm that defines what is to be regarded as "urban" or "metropolitan" while also presenting certain standards and processes for urban planning and design, which have circulated among municipal governments and city councils around the world. The promotion of "soft" location factors, of "quality of life" for elites, and of a prestigious blend of cultural amenities and services for luxury consumption is today part of standard policies for attracting capital investment and highly qualified workers. Accordingly, many contemporary cities both in the global North and in the global South have been equipped with skyscrapers, flagship projects, and "star" architecture. The "standard metropolitan architecture" is becoming the new fuel of global urbanisation. In this context, a remarkable shift in models for the "urban future" has taken place. Today, "new" metropolises such as Dubai, Shanghai, and Singapore are much more likely to be seen as models for the future of urban development than the "old" Western metropolises such as Paris or New York (Roy 2008). As an effect of these policies, processes of gentrification and of urban upgrading are spreading on a global scale, into the cities of the South, into suburban areas, and even into smaller cities. These trends also entail a significant rescaling of urban development. Processes of gentrification and displacement are no longer limited to individual neighbourhoods; rather, entire intra-urban areas and even large parts of metropolitan regions are upgraded and transformed into zones of reproduction for metropolitan elites. A massive increase in land and real estate prices and the accompanying housing crisis have already imposed heavy restrictions on access to these areas for less privileged sections of the population. In order to learn more about these processes, INURA started a collective mapping project which traces the various elements of the new metropolitan mainstream in more than thirty cities, bringing together scientists, professionals and practitioners. Initial results were presented at an exhibition in conjunction with the 20th INURA conference held in Zurich in 2010 (see inura.org).

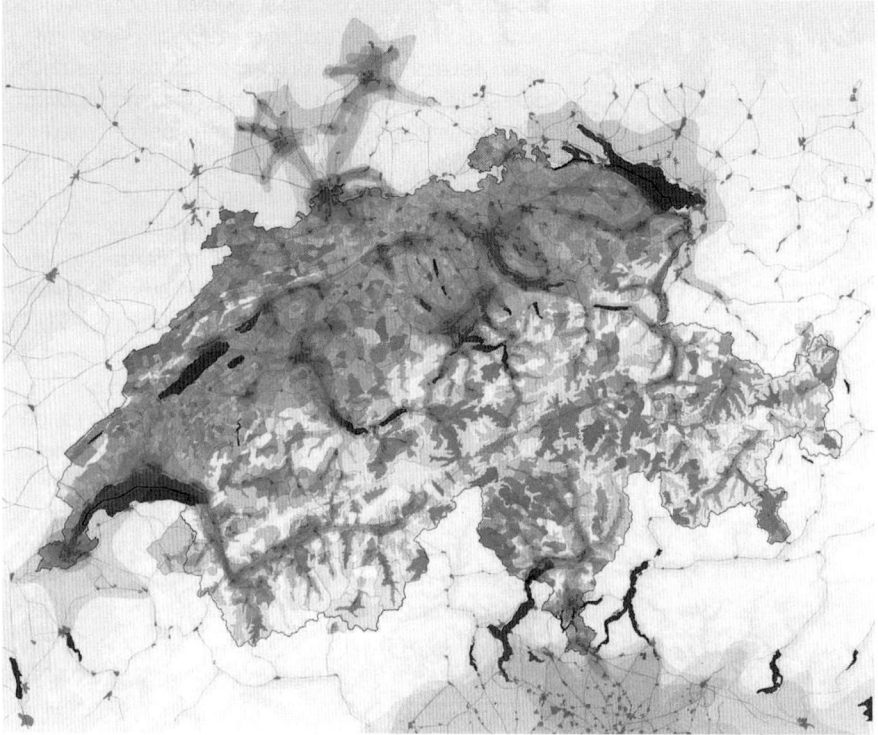

The urban map of Switzerland.
source: Diener et al. (2005), *Switzerland—an Urban Portrait.* Basel: Birkhäuser.

fig. 4

Switzerland—An Urban Portrait. A different approach and methodological design was applied in the *Switzerland—An Urban Portrait* project (Diener 2005 et al.). The aim of this research was not primarily to compare individual cities, but to analyse the urbanisation of the territory and the contemporary urban condition of Switzerland. The theoretical and methodological framework developed in this project makes it possible to detect different forms of urbanisation and urban potential. The theoretical starting point was Henri Lefebvre's famous hypothesis on the complete urbanisation of society, already put forward in 1970 (Lefebvre 2003). This hypothesis involves a decisive change in analytical perspective, from the classical distinction between urban and rural areas, which have been dominant in urban theory for such a long time (see Simmel 1971, Wirth 1938), towards a study of the differences taking shape in the urban world.

(☞ fig. 4)

The study put forth three elementary criteria for determining and analysing today's urban phenomena: networks, borders, and differences. On the basis of these criteria, it was possible to describe the entire territory in urban terms and to develop a typology of urbanized areas in Switzerland: "metropolitan regions", "network cities", "quiet zones", "Alpine resorts" and "Alpine fallow lands".

With this analysis, it is also possible to compare individual cities, such as the metropolitan region of Zurich and the Région Lémanique, around Lake Geneva with the two main centres Geneva and Lausanne. These two regions show very diverse features and properties. If mapped appropriately, this diversity becomes visible. The project constructed different layers (including built-up areas, transport systems, commuters' routes, etc.) which were overlapped and resulted in an approximate shape of the regions. If these patterns are compared, it is clear that they are very different, and these differences have considerable effects on

02 h 30 min

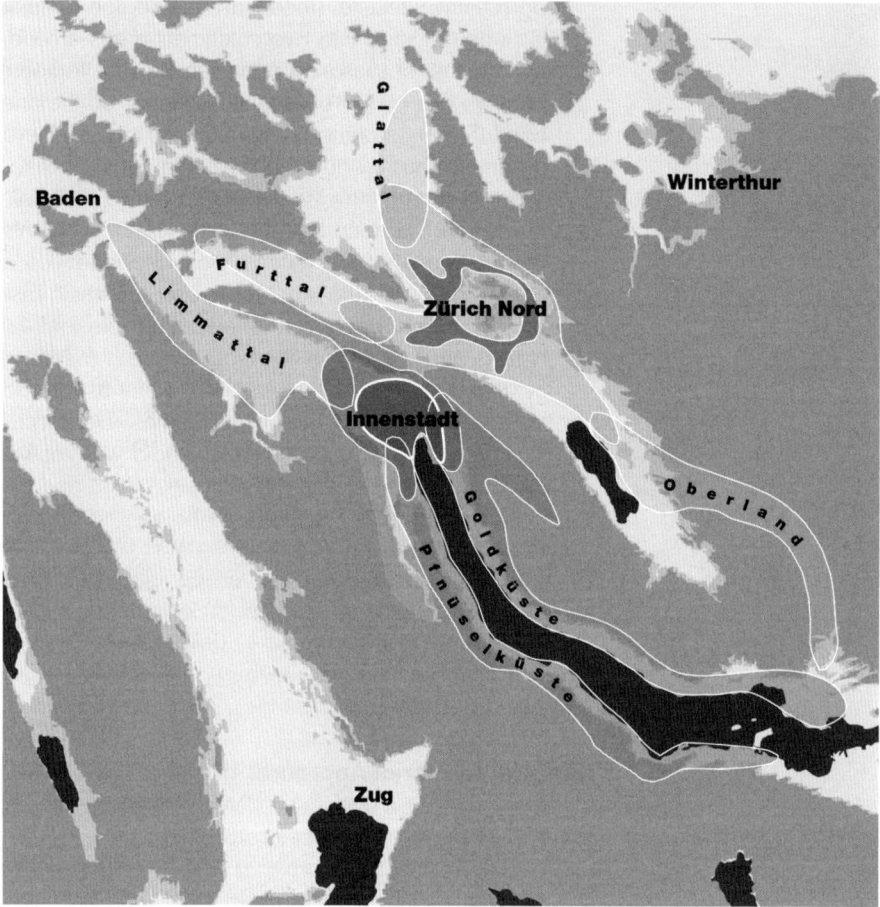

Region Zürich: urban configurations.
source: Diener et al. (2005), *Switzerland—an Urban Portrait*. Basel: Birkhäuser.

The map contains the following labels: Glattal, Baden, Winterthur, Furttal, Limmattal, Zürich Nord, Innenstadt, Goldküste, Pfnüselküste, Oberland, Zug.

fig. 5

(☞ fig. 5)

daily life. Zurich is characterised by urban sprawl and reveals a strong regional dimension and a complex polycentric structure. In contrast, the Région Lémanique is clearly divided into two catchment areas around the two centres of Lausanne and Geneva. The region of Geneva has a very unusual urban form: on the one hand there is a compact monocentric city, on the other an amorphous urban area stretching out into France, separated from the city of Geneva by the national border and a green belt. Nevertheless, this urbanised area is in everyday life completely dependent on and oriented towards the city of Geneva, it forms a reservoir for cheap labour and offers affordable land for houses and villas. Thus the map reveals a hidden reality, which everybody knows but which was for a long time not addressed in political debates. Geneva has thus developed two sides: the splendid well-known international city oriented towards the lake, and the neglected backside beyond the border, hardly connected with the city—"l'autre Genève".

(☞ fig. 6)

This analysis of the patterns of urbanisation presents a snapshot of the current situation. It is of course crucial to understand why and how these patterns developed. This refers to a historical analysis of the dynamics of urbanisation processes.

A Historical Territorial Approach. This historical analysis was carried out within the framework of an interdisciplinary research project involving architects, geographers and historians, which also included a comparative analysis of Zurich and Geneva (see Marco et al. 1997). The project was based on the regulation approach, which was theoretically extended towards a territorial dimension. At the heart of this is the concept of the "territorial relation" (*rapport territorial*) that defines the specific field of regulation of the territory (Schmid 1996).

The main instrument applied in this research was

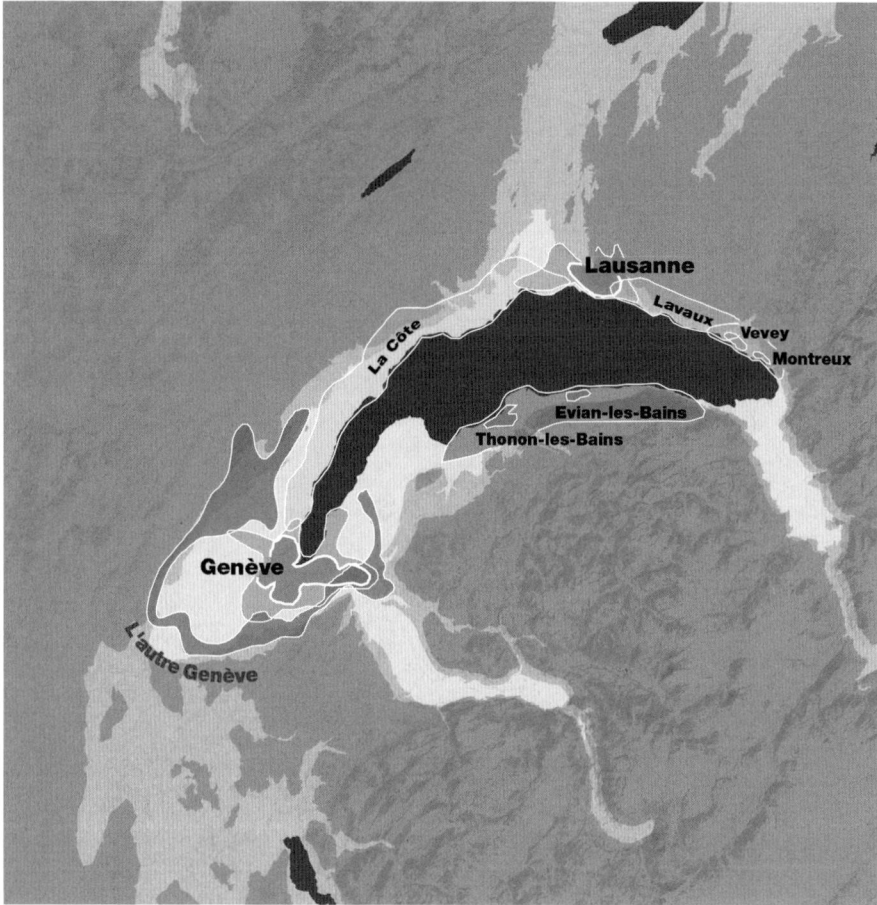

Région Lémanique: urban configurations.
source: Diener et al. (2005), *Switzerland—an Urban Portrait*. Basel: Birkhäuser.

fig. 6

periodisation in order to compare the individual models of urbanisation and to identify the specificity of their trajectories. Periodisation has long been developed and applied in the social sciences and has, for example, entered discussions on Fordism and post-Fordism (Lipietz 1996). However, in the context of comparing urban development, the challenge consists in analysing local trajectories, which are articulated with superordinate cycles but nevertheless show a certain degree of independence. Furthermore, periodisation should be able to address the processes of urbanisation, and this means distinguishing various phases of the production of space. While these are linked to more general social processes, they follow a logic of their own and accordingly display a different kind of dynamic.

It is not possible to go into the details of this analysis, but one result was striking: it turned out that the beginning of the urbanisation process in the early nineteenth century had a decisive impact on the further development of both cities. At that time, Zurich was a relatively small city of about 10,000 inhabitants, which had a certain political power, but was economically not very important. However, it was located in the centre of the most industrialized region of Switzerland and thus soon became the very centre of this industrialized region and the largest city in Switzerland. Until today, Zurich is particularly oriented towards this region and forms an important centre of even global reach. Geneva however developed differently. At the beginning of the nineteenth century, it was by far the largest city in Switzerland with about 25,000 inhabitants. It formed a Protestant city-state with almost no territory. Outside the city walls was the "enemy": a predominantly Catholic and rural population. Thus, Geneva represented in many respects the opposite model to Zurich—and both cities still today display these fundamental differences.

This example clearly shows how the historic pathway of urban development is engraved upon the territory, and how patterns of urbanisation survive, influencing urbanisation processes up to the present time. This leads to a twofold analysis: an analysis of the patterns of urbanisation, and an analysis of the pathways of urbanisation. This concept can now be further developed.

Three Dimensions of Urbanisation. According to Henri Lefebvre's theory of the production of space, the urbanisation process can be analysed in three dimensions: first, the production of material elements and structures; second, the processes of regulation and representation; and third, socialisation and learning processes (Lefebvre 1991, Schmid 2008).

Material structures: first of all, urban space is perceived space. As such, it is a space of material interaction that is opened up by all kinds of networks and information flows. Interaction processes are inscribed upon the urban space; they form shapes and patterns, from the earliest dirt trails to modern-day fibre-optic networks. This aspect of the material production of space has already been clearly conceptualised by David Harvey (1985) as the production of the built environment. Harvey also identified the main contradiction of this production process: the contradiction between fixity and motion (Brenner 1998): in order to allow movements in space it is necessary to produce the necessary infrastructure (like high-speed trains, airports etc.) which is fixed in space. In economic terms, this requires massive long-term investments which have great influence on later development. Once decisions on such infrastructures are taken, they establish the material bases of nodes and networks and thus also define centralities and peripheries on all scales. It needs a huge effort to change these structures and they therefore survive for a very long time. These mate-

Christian Schmid

rial structures are deeply embedded in the city, and they have massive effects on everyday life, for they define the lines along which the urban fabric takes shape, thus influencing future development.

Regulation and representation: second, the city can be analysed as a conceived space or a representation of space. The common understanding of what a city is depends upon the social definition of urban space. If we ask somebody in Paris and somebody else in Los Angeles to define the city, we will get quite different answers. These answers are strongly influenced by the dominant concepts of space, and thus by the image of the city, the blueprint or the map, and also by the plan that attempts to define and pin down the characteristics of urban space. All these various definitions are specific representations of space. They describe discursive demarcations of the content of urban space and entail corresponding strategies of inclusion and exclusion. Definitions of the city become a field in which a variety of strategies and interests come together. These take the form of explicit and implicit procedures and rules that regulate the process of urbanisation in a particular way. Representations of space thus are related to power and define how space is used and reproduced. Finally, they not only determine how we discuss, but also how we act.

Socialisation and learning processes: third, the city is always a lived space as well—a place of residents, who use it and appropriate it in their everyday practices. Urban space can be identified as the place of difference: its specific quality comes from the simultaneous presence of quite distinct worlds and concepts of value, of ethnic, cultural, and social groups, and of activities, functions, and knowledge. Urban space establishes the possibility of bringing all these diverse elements together and making them productive. At the same time, however, there is also a tendency for the elements to cut themselves off and become separate.

How these differences are experienced in actual daily life is crucial. The qualities of urban space are embedded in our history and in our everyday experiences, and are a result of socialisation processes which are always contextualised in concrete places. Thus, processes of socialisation and learning play a decisive role in determining the shape of everyday life in a city.

Models of Urbanisation. These three basic concepts can be applied to the analysis of the contemporary urban process, making it apparent that urbanity and urban qualities do not come about automatically as a result of urbanisation. While urbanisation lays the groundwork for the generation of urban situations, these are only created as a result of the interplay of multiple actions. Urbanisation is always a physical process shaped by specific local conditions, structures, and constellations. Therefore, the process of global urbanisation does not necessarily imply that the entirety of urban space becomes homogenous. Quite the contrary, for many differences within the urban space are increasing (Herzog and de Meuron 2007).

Accordingly, in different places, different local cultures of urbanity and thus various models of urbanisation have evolved. Individual urbanisation models are determined by a wide range of historical experiences, traditions, beliefs, and value systems. They are transmitted as commonly accepted collective processes of socialisation and learning, with the built environment playing an important role as the material basis of everyday experience. These urban cultures are local: while many conditions of urbanisation are proceeding on a national or even global scale, fundamental differences in the models of urbanisation can frequently be found even within a single country. The examples of New York, Los Angeles and Chicago, of Toronto, Montreal and Vancouver, of Milan, Rome and Naples, and even of Zurich, Geneva and Basel provide enough evidence to support such a thesis.

In order to understand such differences, we must often look back over a long period, for the cultures of urbanisation are deeply inscribed in the history of a territory. Just as, conversely, history constantly inscribes itself anew in the territory. During this process, earlier strata are not obliterated, but rather tend to be over-written, as with a palimpsest. A great variety of urban cultures are developing, resulting in different models of urbanisation. It is crucial to understand their origins, their pathways of development, and their possible impacts, in order to detect and explore the specific urban potentials they contain.

How can models of urbanisation be analysed? The problem we face today is that cities no longer con-stitute units that can be delimited; they are highly dy-namic, multifaceted and complex. A twofold approach is required in order to grasp these factors: on one hand, a "horizontal", synchronic analysis is needed which starts from the current situation of the territory, determines the expansion of and interaction between urban regions, and reveals variations in the process of urbanisation. On the other hand, urban development has to be understood and conceived of as a historical production process. This requires a historical, "verti-cal", diachronic analysis. Only through a combination of both perspectives can the specificity of an urban region be identified and understood.

Patterns of Urbanisation. Horizontal analysis examines the structure of the city and urban situations as they are at a given moment. While increasingly exact data and detailed methods are available for analysing the structure of a city, experience has shown that, in most cases, precise mapping of spatial phenomena and distributions can only create an appearance of exactness. Urbanisation is a complex process that is constantly changing shape. Therefore, no given repre-

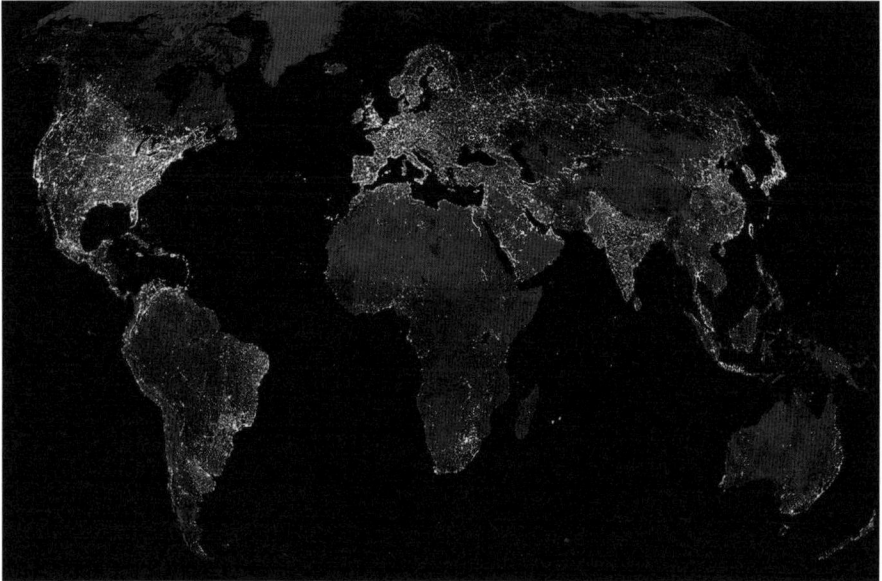

Global urbanisation: light emissions at night.
source: NASA, Goddard Space Flight Center, Scientific Visualization Studio, (2004).

fig. 7

sentation can provide more than just a snapshot. Furthermore, urban reality comprises very diverse attributes that are superimposed in layers. Accordingly, many different lines of demarcation can be drawn, depending on the observer's perspective and heuristic interest. Worldwide light emission at night is one of the possible images that illustrate the patterns of global urbanisation. In fact this photograph does not grasp urbanisation directly, but shows rather a form of pollution, namely light pollution. It serves here as an illustration or a metaphor, to show how urbanised areas are seen from the outside. It has indeed been used as an indicator for the delimitation of urban mega regions (Florida et al. 2008). It was also one of the main components of the construction of "urban extents", or built-up urban areas on a global scale (see Balk et al. 2004). On both maps it becomes visible that there are tremendous differences in the patterns of urbanisation around the globe already on a large scale. The analysis now needs to look closer at these patterns, and ask how they are produced, what they imply and what the concrete local effects are.

(☞ fig. 7)

(☞ fig. 8)

This analysis also needs to address the question of scale: urban realities are on different scales, and the various urban networks differ in terms of their spatial expansion and are superimposed upon one another. At the top end of the scale are vast megalopolises or "urban galaxies" (Gottman 1961; Soja and Kanai 2007), whose expansion is "continental". At the next level are urban mega-regions or conurbations (Florida et al. 2008), which are large considerably urbanized networked spaces. Examples include Greater Tokyo, but also the Swiss Plateau. These urban mega-regions can again be structured quite heterogeneously within themselves, and may include various agglomerations, metropolitan regions, or networks of cities, but also large green spaces and sparsely settled zones (Diener et al. 2005). Individual regions may again be

Global urbanisation: urban extents.
source: Global Rural-Urban Mapping Project, alpha Data, Columbia University—New York, (2005).

fig. 8

structured quite heterogeneously within themselves—their structure may be monocentric, bipolar, or polycentric—and may be composed of various urban configurations. It is important to look at the interference of the different scales and to go up and down with the analysis. (☞ page 79, Neil Brenner)

Pathways of Urbanisation. On the basis of the horizontal analysis, a vertical, historical analysis should follow. It descends into the past to identify the defining moments of urban culture that have inscribed themselves into the terrain and collective memory. Subsequently, the analysis must ascend in order to attempt to reconstruct the decisive lines of development and to draft a timeline oriented along the respective dominant constellations of power and the most important fields of conflict. In particular, it is crucial to identify the constants and the discontinuities in the development.

This analysis does not simply aim to reconstruct the history of a city, but is intended to detect the ways in which history remains present in the contemporary situation and influences future developments. The aim is to understand the path dependency of urban areas. As Lefebvre pointed out, no social space disappears completely, because it forms the starting point for subsequent development. Every social space therefore survives in one form or another. It will leave traces that may be visible or hidden: monuments, urban structures, or even specific symbols survive, albeit often in seclusion, but they remain effective. It is important to conduct an exact analysis of these historic aspects.

If we look at the pathways of urban development we can see that they are also very different. One possible illustration of these differences is the graphic representation of the population growth of metropolitan areas. Again, such a diagram serves merely as an illustration of the highly complex underlying urbanisation processes involved in urban transformations.

The Urban as Open Horizon. All the examples presented above show very different ways of comparing urban development and urban experiences, and they reveal certain basic qualities of contemporary urbanisation. The urbanisation process itself, as we have seen, is not homogenising but it is rather differentiating and highly path-dependent.

Urbanisation always implies that global tendencies are materialising in local contexts. This materialisation is accomplished accordingly to the specificities of the place, and therefore urbanisation is not just determined by global forces, but it is also a process of inventing, because this clash of global tendencies with the "local" leads to the creation of new forms. Urbanisation could thus be understood as a constant struggle for new solutions and a search for new spatial forms. The result is often unpredictable and full of surprises. We should therefore not just look at urban forms, but rather at urbanisation processes and their rhythms: a certain form identified and analysed today might be completely transformed or may even have disappeared in a few years' time.

The "city" is not a general category, but a concrete, historical one that is constantly being redefined. The general trends of urbanisation are materialized in various different ways in particular locations. Urbanisation is always a concrete process shaped by specific local conditions, structures, and constellations. Therefore, the process of global urbanisation in no way implies that all urban space must become homogenous. Quite the contrary, for differences within urban areas are increasing.

Comparative analysis can help give a better understanding of the local conditions in which global processes materialise and it can thus help us explore the possibilities and potentials that we might expect for future developments.

Christian Schmid

This text serves as a theoretical and conceptual basis for the Global Urbanisation in Comparative Perspective research project of the Future Cities Laboratory of the Singapore—ETH Centre for Global Environmental Sustainability. It integrates the results of the USUM WP2 research. Sincere thanks are due especially to Pascal Kallenberger, Anne Schmidt and Monika Streule who formed the USUM WP2 research team for Patterns and Pathways of Global Urbanisation and greatly contributed to the drafting of this paper.

Bibliography
1. Abu-Lughod, J. L. (1999), *New York, Chicago, Los Angeles: America's Global Cities.* Minneapolis: University of Minnesota Press.
2. Angel, S., Sheppard S. C. and Civco, D. L. (2005), *The Dynamics of Global Urban Expansion.* Washington.
3. Balk, D., Pozzi, F., Yetman, G., Deichmann, U. and Nelson, A. (2004), *The Distribution of People and the Dimension of Place: Methodologies to Improve the Global Estimation of Urban Extents* (paper). CIESIN—Columbia University New York, the World Bank and the University of Leeds.
4. Boeri, S. et al. (2000), Multiplicity: Uncertain States of Europe. In Koolhaas, R. et al., *Mutations,* . Bordeaux: ACTAR / arc en rêve, page 338—483.
5. Boudreau, J., A., Hamel, P., Jouve, B. and Keil, R. (2007), New State Spaces in Canada: Metropolitanisation in Montreal and Toronto Compared. In *Urban Geography* 28 (1), page 30—53.
6. Brenner, N. (1998), Between Fixity and Motion: Accumulation, Territorial Organization and the Historical Geography of Spatial Scales. In *Environmental and Planning D: Society and Space* 16 (4), page 459—481.
7. Brenner, N. (2001), World City Theory, Globalization and the Comparative—Historical Method: Reflections on Janet Abu-Lughod's Interpretation of Contemporary Urban Restructuring. In *Urban Affairs Review* 36 (6), page 124-147.

8. Brenner, N. and Keil, R. (2006), *The Global Cities Reader*. New York: Routledge.

9. Brenner, N. and Schmid, S. (2012). Planetary Urbanisation. In Gandy, M., *Urban Constellations*, Berlin: Jovis (forthcoming).

10. Brenner, N. and Theodore, N. (2002), *Spaces of Neoliberalism: Urban Restructuring in Western Europe and North America*. Oxford and Boston: Blackwell.

11. Brillembourg, A., Feireiss, K. and Klumpner, H. (2005), *Informal City: Caracas Case*. Munich: Prestel Verlag.

12. Burdett, R. and Ichioka, S. (2006), *10ᵗʰ International Architecture Exhibition: Cities, Architecture, and Society*, vol. 1. Verona: Marsilio.

13. Burdett, R. and Sudjic, D. (2007), *The Endless City: The Urban Age Project*. London: Phaidon Press.

14. Davis, D. E. (2005). Cities in Global Context: A Brief Intellectual History. In *International Journal of Urban and Regional Research* 29 (1), page 92—109.

15. Davis, M. (2006), *Planet of Slums*. London: Verso

16. Diener, R., Herzog J., Meili, M., de Meuron, P. and Schmid, C. (2005), *Switzerland—an Urban Portrait*. Basel: Birkhäuser.

17. Florida, R., Gulden, T. and Mellander, C. (2008), The Rise of the Mega-Region. In *Cambridge Journal of Regions, Economy and Society* 1 (3), page 459—476.

18. Friedmann, J. (1986), The World City Hypothesis. In *Development and Change* 17 (1), page 69—84.

19. Garreau, J. (1991), *Edge City: Life on the New Frontier*. New York: Doubleday.

20. Gottman, J. (1961), *Megalopolis: The Urbanised Northeastern Seaboard of the United States*. New York: The Twentieth Century Fund.

21. Gugler, J. (1997), *Cities In the Developing World: Issues, Theory and Policy*. Oxford: Oxford University Press.

22. Hall, P. and Pain, K. (2006), *The Polycentric Metropolis. Learning From Mega-City Regions in Europe*. London: Earthscan.

23. Harvey, D. (1985), *The Urbanisation of Capital: Studies in the History and Theory of Capitalist Urbanisation 2*. Oxford: Blackwell.

24. Herzog, J. and de Meuron, P. (2007), The Particular and the Generic. In Burdett, R. and Sudjic, D., *The Endless City*, New York: Phaidon Press Inc., page 324—327.

25. Hitz, H., Keil, R., Lehrer, U., Ronneberger, K., Schmid, C. and Wolff, R. (1995). *Capitales Fatales: Urbanisierung und Politik in den Finanzmetropolen Frankfurt und Zürich*. Zürich: Rotpunkt.

26. INURA and Palosicia, R. (2004), *The Contested Metropolis. Six Cities at the Beginning of the 21ˢᵗ Century*. Berlin: Birkhäuser.

27. Kantor, P. (2008), Varieties of City Regionalism and the Quest for Political Cooperation: A Comparative Perspective. In *Urban Research and Practice* 1 (2), page 111—129.

28. Koolhaas R. (1978), *Delirious New York: A Retroactive Manifesto for Manhattan*. Oxford: Oxford University Press.

29. Lang, R. E. (2003), *Edgeless Cities: Exploring the Elusive Metropolis*. Washington DC: Brookings Institutions Press.

30. Lévy, Jacques et al. (2008), *L'invention Du Monde: Une Géographie De La Mondialisation*. Paris: Sciences Po Press.

31. Lefebvre, H. (1991), *The Production of Space*. Oxford: Blackwell Press.

32. Lefebvre, H. (2003), *The Urban Revolution*. Minneapolis: University of Minnesota Press.

33. Lipietz, A. (1996), *La société en sablier. Le partage du travail contre la déchirure sociale*. Paris: La Découverte.

34. Marco, D., Schmid, C., Hirschi, C., Hiler, D. and Capol, J. (1997), *La ville: villes de crise ou crise des villes. Rapport scientifique final pour le 'Fonds national suisse de la recherche scientifique'*. Institut d'Architecture de l'Université de Genève.

35. Marcuse, P. and van Kempen, R. (2000), *Globalizing Cities: A New Spatial Order?* Malden and Mass: Blackwell.

36. Moulaert, F., Rodriguez, A. and Swyngedouw, E. (2003), *The Globalized City—Economic Restructuring and Social Polarization in European Cities*. Oxford: University Press Oxford.

Christian Schmid

37. Neuwirth, R. (2005), *Shadow Cities: A Billion Squatters, a New Urban World*. New York: Routledge.

38. Nijman, J. (2007), Introduction: Comparative Urbanism. In *Urban Geography* 28 (1), page 1—6.

39. Oswalt, P. et al. (2006), *Atlas of Shrinking Cities*. Ostfildern-Ruit: Hatje Cantz.

40. Park, R. E., Burgess, E. W. and McKenzie, R. D. (1925), *The City*. Chicago: The University of Chicago Press.

41. Porter, L. and Shaw, K. (2009), *Whose Urban Renaissance? An International Comparison of Urban Regeneration Strategies*. London: Routledge.

42. Robinson, J. (2006), *Ordinary Cities: Between Modernity and Development*. London and New York: Routledge.

43. Roy, A. (2008), The 21st Century Metropolis: New Geographies of Theory. In *Regional Studies* 42 (1), page 1—12.

44. Roy, A. and AlSayyad, N. (2004), *Urban Informality: Transnational Perspectives from Latin America, the Middle East, and South Asia*. New York: Lexington Books.

45. Sassen, S. (1991), *The Global City: New York, London, Tokyo*. Princeton: Princeton University Press.

46. Schmid, C. (1996). Urbane Region und Territorialverhältnis: Zur Regulation des Urbanisierungsprozesses. In Bruch, M. and Krebs, H-P., *Unternehmen Globus—Facetten nachfordistischer Regulation*. Münster: Westfälisches Dampfboot, page 224—253.

47. Schmid, C. (2005), *Stadt, Raum und Gesellschaft: Henri Lefebvre und die Theorie der Produktion des Raumes*. Stuttgart: Franz Steiner Verlag.

48. Schmid, C. (2008), Henri Lefebvre's Theory of the Production of Space: Towards a Three-Dimensional Dialectic. In Goonewardena, K. et al., *Space, Difference, Everyday Life: Reading Henri Lefebvre*. London: Routledge, page 27—45.

49. Schmid, C. (2011), Henri Lefebvre, the Right to the City and the New Metropolitan Mainstream. In Brenner, N. Marcuse, P. and Mayer, M., *Cities for People, not for Profit: Critical Urban Theory and the Right to the City*. London and New York: Routledge, page 42—62.

50. Scott, A. J. (2000), *Global City-Regions: Trends, Theory, Policy*. Oxford: Oxford University Press.

51. Scott, A. J. and Soja, E. W. (1996), *The City: Los Angeles and Urban Theory at the End of the Twentieth Century*. Berkeley and Los Angeles: University of California Press.

52. Sieverts, T. (2003), *Cities Without Cities: An Interpretation of the Zwischenstadt*. London: Spon Press.

53. Simone, A. M. (2004), *For the City yet to Come: Changing African Life in Four Cities*. Durham NC: Duke University Press.

54. Simmel, G. (1971), The Metropolis and Mental Life, In Levine, D.N., *Georg Simmel on Individuality and Social Forms*. Chicago and London: The University of Chicago Press, page 324—339.

55. Smith, N. (2002), New Globalism, New Urbanism: Gentrification as Global Strategy. In Brenner, N. and Theodore, N., *Spaces of Neoliberalism: Urban Restructuring in North America and Western Europe*. London: Blackwell, page 80—103.

56. Soja, E. W. (1992), Inside Exopolis: Scenes From Orange County. In Sorkin , M., *Variations on a Theme Park*. New York: The Noonday Press, page 94—122.

57. Soja, E. W. and Kanai, M. (2007), The Urbanisation of the World. In Burdett, R. and Sudjic, D., *The Endless City*. New York: Phaidon Press Inc., page 54—69.

58. Swyngedouw, E. A. (1997), Neither Global nor Local: Glocalization and the Politics of Scale. In Cox, K., *Spaces of Globalization*. New York and London: Guilford, page 137—166.

59. Taylor, P. J. (2004), *World City Network: A Global Urban Analysis*. London and New York: Routledge.

60. Taylor, P. J. and Lang, R. (2004). The Shock of the New: 100 Concepts Describing Recent Urban Change. In *Environment and Planning A* 36 (6), page. 951-958.

61. Venturi, R. , Scott Brown, D. and Izenour S. (1972), *Learning from Las Vegas: The Forgotten Symbolism of Architectural Form*. Cambridge MA: MIT Press.

62. Ward, K. (2008), Towards a Comparative (Re)Turn in Urban Studies? Some Reflections. In *Urban Geography* 29 (5), page 405—410.

63. Wirth, L. (1938), Urbanism as a Way of Life. In *The American Journal of Sociology* 44 (1), p. 1—24.

64. Wu, F. and Phelps, N. (2008), From Suburbia to Post-Suburbia in China? Aspects of the Transformation of the Beijing and Shanghai Global City Regions. In *Built Environment* 34 (4), page. 464—481.

Neil Brenner, is Professor of Urban Theory at the Harvard GSD—Graduate School of Design. His research areas include global and comparative urban development, critical urban theory, comparative-historical geopolitical economy, and state theory.

Rescaling the urban question. Since the early

1990s, there has been an explosion of social-scientific interest in the dual problematic of "scale" and "rescaling." First, it is now widely recognized that the scalar constitution of modern capitalism—its differentiation among local, regional, national, transnational, and global geographical units—is not a pregiven feature of social life but is, rather, historically produced and contested. (☞ page 89, Reference1) Second, key contributions to geopolitical economy, state theory, urban studies, social movement studies and environmental geography have drawn attention to diverse forms of contemporary scalar transformation, or rescaling, in which inherited scalar arrangements are being challenged and reworked. (☞ Ref.2) Whereas the social sciences have long contained implicit assumptions regarding the scalar constitution of political-economic processes, these more recent interdisciplinary developments indicate that the "scale question" is now being confronted with an unprecedented methodological reflexivity.

Here, I draw upon this newly consolidated literature to conceptualize the changing character of what has come to be known as the "urban question." The urban question has a complex lineage within the twentieth century social sciences, but it was first labeled as such in the early 1970s by M. Castells; and it has subsequently been debated extensively by urbanists and social theorists alike. (☞ Ref.3) I argue that post-1980s scalar transformations require a fundamental rethinking of the urban question. Although I do not believe that the contemporary urban question can be grasped entirely with reference to scalar transformations, I will suggest that the latter have fundamentally altered the geographical and institutional terrain on which the process of urban development is unfolding. Thus the urban question and the scale question are today intertwined in ways that require sustained theoretical, methodological, and empirical scrutiny.

Since the early 1970s, debates on the urban question have centered on the conceptualization of space in research on cities. (☞ Ref.4) However, in their efforts to conceptualize urban spatiality, urban theorists have necessarily introduced diverse assumptions concerning the distinctiveness of the urban scale of sociospatial organization (as opposed to, for instance, regional, national or global scales). To unpack this assertion and its implications for contemporary urban theory, I reconstruct briefly some of the distinctive scalar assumptions upon which previous rounds of debate on the urban question have been grounded.

The 1970s: the functional specificity of the urban. In his classic work *The Urban Question* (1977 [1972]), Manuel Castells attacked the Chicago school of urban sociology for its failure to grasp the historical specificity of the urban form under capitalism. Against this universalistic "urban ideology," Castells set out to delimit the role of the "urban system" as a determinate structure within the capitalist mode of production. In so doing, Castells implicitly distinguished two basic dimensions of the urban, which for present purposes can be termed its scalar and its functional aspects. The scalar aspect of the urban concerned the materiality of social processes organized on the urban scale as opposed to supraurban scales. In Castells' terminology, scales are understood as the differentiated "spatial units" of which the capitalist system is composed. (☞ Ref.5) The functional aspect of the urban, Castells' most explicit focus in *The Urban Question*, concerned not merely the geographical setting or territorial scope of social processes but their functional role or "social content." (☞ Ref.6) According to Castells' famous argument, the specificity of the urban "spatial unit" could be delimited theoretically neither with reference to its ideological, its political-juridical nor its production functions, but only in terms of its role as a site for the reproduction of labor-power. (☞ Ref.7) Castells repeatedly acknowledged the existence of multiple social processes within capitalist cities, but argued that only collective consumption was functionally specific to the urban scale. The essence of Castells' position, then, was the attempt to define geographical scale in terms of its social function.

Castells began to modify this position almost immediately after the publication of *The Urban Question*, but the book continued to exercise a strong influence upon conceptualizations of geographical scale within urban studies. (☞ Ref.8) Peter Saunders' critique of Castells' early work usefully illustrates the extent of this influence. (☞ Ref.9) The core of Saunders' critique of Castells was a rejection of the notion that any of the social processes located within cities are, in a necessary sense, functionally specific to that geographical scale. This observation led Saunders to view urban spatial organization as a merely contingent effect, and thus as a flawed conceptual basis for confronting the urban question. In reaching this conclusion, however, Saunders implicitly embraced Castells' own criterion of functional specificity as the theoretical linchpin to the urban question. It was this underlying assumption that enabled Saunders to invoke the supraurban character of the social processes located within cities as grounds for dismissing the possibility of a coherent spatial definition of the urban. Saunders' alternative proposal to define urban sociology as the study of consumption processes preserved the label "urban" only as a "matter of convention." (☞ Ref.10) Saunders thereby rendered the urban dimension of urban sociology entirely accidental, a random choice of geographical scale.

Despite their opposed conclusions, both positions in the Castells/Saunders debate were premised on two shared assumptions regarding the role of geographical scale in the urban question. First, both authors viewed the urban scale as the self-evident empirical centerpiece of the urban question. Because of their overarching concern with the functional content of the urban, Castells and Saunders reduced its scalar dimension to a pregiven empirical fact. Consequently, neither author could explicitly analyze the ways in which the urban scale is itself socially produced or, most crucially from the vantage point of the post-1980s period, the possibility of its historical transformation. Second, the arguments of both Castells and Saunders were grounded on what might be termed a "zero-sum" conception of geographical scale—the notion that scales operate as mutually exclusive rather than as co-constitutive territorial frameworks for social relations.

On this basis, both Castells and Saunders implied that supraurban geographical scales were merely external parameters for the urban question. By contrast, the inter-linkages between urban and supraurban scales have today become intrinsic to the very content of the urban question.

The 1980s: from scale-specificity to the production of space. Various alternatives to Castells' early work were elaborated during the late 1970s and early 1980s, as many urban scholars attempted to redefine the specificity of the urban. The key task from this perspective was to delineate social processes that were tied intrinsically, but not exclusively, to the urban scale. Thus cities were now analyzed as multidimensional geographical sites in which, for instance, industrial production, local labor markets, infrastructural configurations, inter-firm relations, urban land-use systems, and consumption processes were clustered together. From David Harvey's capital-theoretic account of urban built environments and Allen J. Scott's neo-Ricardian theorization of the urban land nexus to Michael Storper and Richard Walker's post-Weberian analysis of industrial agglomeration and territorial development, these approaches replaced Castells' criterion of functional specificity with that of scale-specificity. (☞ Ref.11) The analytical core of the urban question was no longer the functional unity of the urban process but rather the role of the urban scale as a multifaceted geographical materialization of capitalist social relations. In effect, Castells' early position was inverted. Against his conception of scales as the spatial expressions of social functions, the social relations of capitalism were now analyzed in terms of their distinctive patterns of agglomeration and territorialization on the urban scale. These multifaceted analyses of urban spatiality soon flowed into broader explorations of the production of space and spatial configuration under capitalism. David Harvey's historical-geographical materialist conceptualization of the spatial fix exemplified this tendency. In his writings of the 1980s, Harvey continued to view the urban scale as a key geographical foundation for the accumulation process and elaborated a periodization of capitalist development focused on successive historical forms of urbanisation. (☞ Ref.12) At the same time, Harvey began more explicitly to conceptualize the role of supraurban spaces and processes—for example, regional divisions of labor, national institutional constellations, supranational regimes of accumulation, and world market conditions—as central geographical preconditions for each historical spatial fix under capitalism. Closely analogous methodological strategies were elaborated by other scholars such as Doreen Massey, Neil Smith, and Ed Soja, who embedded a discussion of the urban question within an account of capitalist spatiality on supraurban scales, whether with reference to changing spatial divisions of labor, patterns of uneven geographical development, or forms of crisis-induced restructuring.

Three aspects of these debates deserve emphasis here. First, insofar as these analyses of urban spatiality flowed directly into a wide range of supraurban questions-for example, the regional question, the problematic of uneven development, the core-periphery debate, and so forth—the coherence of the urban question was severely unsettled. (☞ Ref.13) Whereas explorations of the urban question had contributed crucially to this broader spatialization of Marxian political economy, the latter trend now appeared to be supplanting the urban question itself, relegating urban space to a mere subtopic within the more general issue of capitalism's uneven global historical geographies. Second, these analyses introduced more multidimensional conceptions of geographical scale than had previously been deployed. Scales were no longer equated with unitary social functions, but were viewed increasingly as crystallizations of diverse, overlapping political-economic processes. Third, despite this methodological advance, the historicity of geographical scales was recognized only in a relatively limited sense. Capital was said to jump continually between the urban, regional, national, and global scales in pursuit of new sources of surplus value, but the possibility that entrenched scalar hierarchies and interscalar relations might themselves be radically transformed was not systematically explored. It was not until the early 1990s, with the proliferation of research on the urban dimensions of economic globalization, that more historically dynamic conceptualizations of geographical scale and interscalar configurations were elaborated within urban studies.

The 1990s and after: urban theory and the globalization debate.

The urban question has continued to provoke intense debate since the 1990s, but its meaning has been redefined in the face of recent geoeconomic and geopolitical transformations. In contrast to previous conceptions of the urban as a relatively self-evident scalar entity, contemporary urban researchers have been confronted with major transformations in the institutional and geographical organization not only of the urban scale but also of the supraurban scalar hierarchies and interscalar networks in which cities are embedded. Under these circumstances, urban researchers have begun to conceptualize the urban question with direct reference to diverse supraurban rescaling processes.

This methodological reorientation can be illustrated briefly with reference to three strands of contemporary urban research. First, world city theorists and industrial geographers have emphasized the enhanced strategic importance of place-specific social relations, localization, and territorial concentration as basic geographical preconditions for global economic transactions. (☞ Ref.14) From this perspective, the urban scale operates as a localized node within globally organized flows, whereas the global scale is in turn constituted through networks of superimposed localities and cities. Second, many authors have analyzed dramatic shifts in both the vertical and horizontal relations among cities, as manifested, for instance, in the consolidation of new global urban hierarchies, in accelerated informational, financial, and migratory flows among cities, in the construction of new planetary interurban telecommunications infrastructures, and in intensified inter-urban competition as well as in countervailing forms of inter-urban cooperation and coordination. (☞ Ref.15) From this perspective, the urban is not only a nested level within supraurban territorial hierarchies but also the product of dense interscalar networks linking dispersed geographical locations. Third, recent regulationist-inspired analyses have linked processes of urban restructuring to various ongoing transformations of state spatial organization that are deprivileging the national regulatory level and giving new importance to both supranational and subnational forms of governance. (☞ Ref.16) From this perspective, the urban scale is not only a localized arena for global capital accumulation but a strategic regulatory coordinate in which a multiscalar restructuring of state spatiality is currently unfolding.

In short, as indicated by the proliferation of terms such as the "local-global interplay," the "local-global nexus," "glocalization," and "glurbanisation," many urban researchers have begun to conceptualize the current round of globalization as a complex rearticulation of socioeconomic space upon multiple geographical scales. The problematic of geographical scale—its spatial organization, its social production, its political contestation, and its historical reconfiguration—has thus been inserted into the very heart of the urban question in the current era. Whereas the urban question had previously assumed the form of debates on the functional specificity or scale-specificity of the urban within relatively stable supraurban territorial configurations, in the 1990s and after, the urban question has been posed increasingly in the form of a scale question.

As evidenced in the diverse fields of urban research mentioned above, a wide range of scholars have suggested that historically entrenched relations among urban and supraurban scales are currently being reorganized. The appropriate interpretation of contemporary global transformations remains open to considerable debate, but three core propositions have been widely embraced among critical urban theorists:

Nationalized scalar fixes are being destabilized. The nationalized formation of capital accumulation, urbanisation, state regulation and sociopolitical struggle—often described as a "scalar fix"—that prevailed throughout the older capitalist world during the Fordist-Keynesian-Bandung period has been seriously destabilized since the mid-1970s. Under contemporary conditions, therefore, the "institutional arrangements that at one time were congruent at the national level are now more dispersed at multiple spatial levels"; meanwhile, a "multifaceted causality runs in virtually all directions among the various levels of society: nations, free trade zones, international regimes, supranational regions, large cities and even small but specialized localities." (☞ Ref.17)

Strategies to reorganize inherited scalar arrangements are proliferating. Consequently, during the last two decades, diverse sociopolitical strategies have been mobilized to reorganize inherited interscalar configurations in key realms of political-economic organization and everyday life, including urbanisation. (☞ Ref.18) Both within and beyond cities, these rescaling strategies are widely viewed as a means to displace or resolve crisis tendencies, to manage regulatory problems, to recalibrate power relations, and to establish a new geographical basis for capitalist development and political-economic governance. In this context, cities and city-regions have become increasingly strategic sites of institutional innovation and sociopolitical contestation.

A relativization of scales is occurring. The medium- and long-term consequences of such rescaling strategies for urban development patterns and everyday city life remain relatively inchoate, but they appear to herald the formation of new interscalar configurations in which the national scale of political-economic organization is no longer hegemonic. This situation has been aptly described by Jessop as a "relativization of scale." (☞ Ref.19) From this point of view, contemporary spatial transformations have not generated a unidirectional process of globalization, triadization, Europeanization, decentralization, regionalization, or localization, in which a single scale-be it global, "triadic," European, regional or local-is replacing the national scale as the primary level of political-economic coordination. What we are witnessing, rather, is a new "scalar flux"-a wide-ranging, contested recalibration of inherited scalar hierarchies and interscalar relations throughout the uneven geographies of global capitalism as a whole. The task of deciphering the tangled scalar hierarchies, mosaics, and networks that have been emerging in the wake of these systemic realignments is still in its embryonic stages, but it is now being confronted by a growing number of interdisciplinary scholars working on diverse aspects of contemporary political-economic and environmental transformations, including urban restructuring. (☞ Ref.20)

Neil Brenner

These theoretical developments have substantially loosened the grip of static, atemporal and unreflexive models of geographical scale on urban research. Nevertheless, despite these accomplishments, significant methodological challenges are associated with the tasks of (a) deciphering the role of cities within contemporary rescaling processes; (b) understanding the implications of rescaling processes for processes of urban development; and (c) theorizing the nature of rescaling processes themselves.

Not least among these challenges is that of constructing an appropriate conceptual grammar for representing the processual, dynamic, and politically contested character of geographical scale and interscalar institutional arrangements. A reification of scale appears to be built into everyday scalar terms (e.g., local, urban, regional, national, global, etc.) insofar as they represent distinctive socio-territorial processes (e.g., localization, urbanisation, regionalization, nationalization, globalization, etc.) as static entities that have been more or less permanently frozen within geographical space. Relatedly, existing scalar vocabularies are poorly equipped to grasp the complex, perpetually changing historical interconnections and interdependencies among geographical scales. Insofar as terms such as "local," "urban," "regional" (and so forth) are used to demarcate purportedly separate territorial "islands" of social relations, they mask the profound mutual imbrication of all scales and the dense interscalar networks through which the latter are continually produced and reconfigured. These difficulties are exacerbated further by the circumstance that much of the social-scientific division of labor is still organized according to distinctive scalar foci—for example, urban studies, regional studies, comparative politics, international relations, etc.—which systematically obstruct efforts to explore the dynamics of interscalar relations and transformations.

Even among those who are concerned to develop a reflexively scale-attuned approach to political economy, the theorization of scale itself has become increasingly contentious. (☞ Ref.21) Theorists differ, for instance, on how best to delineate the essential properties of scale, on the appropriate analytical and empirical scope of the concept, on its relation to other key sociospatial concepts, and on its application to the study of particular empirical phenomena. Clarification of such questions awaits further theoretical debate, methodological experimentation and empirical inquiry by scale-attuned researchers both within, and beyond the field of urban studies.

The proliferation of explicit debates on geographical scale during and after the 1990s can be understood as an important extension and fine-tuning of the spatialized approaches to urban and regional political economy developed during the preceding decade, provoked in no small measure by the post-1970s shaking-up of the scalar hierarchies and interdependencies associated with organized capitalism in a new round of crisis-induced sociospatial restructuring. Subsequently, and not only in urban studies, discussions of the scale question have provided a more precise conceptual grammar for analyzing the continual geographical redifferentiation of sociospatial relations during a particularly volatile period in the geohistory of capitalism. Whereas a sophisticated analytical vocabulary had already been developed in the 1980s for grasping key dimensions of capitalist spatiality-such as localization, the tension between geographical fixity and geographical mobility, the problematic of territoriality, and the phenomenon of uneven spatial development-the new lexicon of geographical scale has provided researchers with a powerful means to denaturalize, historicize, and critically interrogate the very spatial units and hierarchies in which social relations are configured. Consequently, recent debates on the scale question have provided scholars in diverse research fields with an important analytical lens through which to begin to decipher the complex, rapidly changing geographies of contemporary social transformations.

On my reading, recent contributions to the analysis of scale production and scale transformation have particularly massive implications for the field of urban studies, whose unit of analysis remains deeply ambiguous even after nearly a century of debate regarding the nature of the urban question. However, I would caution against the tendency to overextend scalar concepts in urban studies or in any other branch of sociospatial analysis: this is because scalar structurations of social space (based upon relations of hierarchization among vertically differentiated units) are distinct from other forms of sociospatial structuration, such as place-making, localization, territorialization and networking. (☞ Ref.22) The lexicon of geographical scale is most powerful, I have suggested, when its analytical limits are explicitly understood. (☞ Ref.23)

Although capitalism has long been differentiated into scalar hierarchies, the current period of global restructuring is marked by particularly profound transformations of scalar organization. Throughout the last three decades, the geoeconomic project of neoliberalism, with its emphasis on capital mobility, unfettered market relations, and intensified commodification, has entailed a massive assault on established scales of sociopolitical regulation and an aggressive attempt to forge new worldwide scalar hierarchies in which the logic of "beggar-thy-neighbor" competition is to be institutionalized. These trends have had massive ramifications for cities and for urban governance systems, which have become strategic targets for neoliberal projects of spatial and institutional creative destruction. (☞ Ref.24) At the same time, both within and beyond cities, oppositional movements that strive to block or to roll back the contemporary neoliberal onslaught have likewise begun to mobilize geographical scale in strategic, often highly creative ways—whether by "jumping scales" to escape the hegemony of dominant institutional practices, by mobilizing support for reregulatory projects that aim to socialize capital at particular scales, or by envisioning radically different scalar arrangements based on principles of radical democracy, emancipation, and sociospatial justice. In this sense, the increasing prominence of scalar concepts in contemporary social theory and research may be understood as a "real abstraction" of ongoing scalar struggles: it is precisely because the configuration of geographical scale has become such an important stake of contemporary sociopolitical contestation that urbanists and other spatially reflexive social scientists have become so attuned, in recent years, to its profound methodological import.

A previous version of this chapter was published in "New Geographies" (Graduate School of Design, Harvard University), 0, 2008.

Neil Brenner

References
1. Smith, N. (1995), Remaking Scale: Competition and Cooperation in Prenational and Postnational Europe. In Eskelinen, H. and Snickars, F., *Competitive European Peripheries*. Berlin: Springer Verlag, page 59—74; and Swyngedouw, E. (1997), Neither Global nor Local: Glocalization and the Politics of Scale. In Cox, K., *Spaces of Globalization*. New York: Guilford Press, page137—166.
2. Marston, S. A. (2000), The Social Construction of Scale, In *Progress in Human Geography* 24(2), page 219—242.
3. Castells, M. (1977 [1972]), *The Urban Question*, Cambridge, Mass.: MIT Press; and Saunders, P. (1986), *Social Theory and the Urban Question*, New York: Holmes & Meier Publishers; and Katznelson, I. (1993), *Marxism and the City*, New York: Oxford University Press; and Merrifield, A. (2002), *Metromarxism: A Marxist Tale of the City.* New York: Routledge.
4. Gottdiener, M. (1985), *The Social Production of Urban Space.* Austin: University of Texas Press.
5. Castells, *The Urban Question*, op. cit., page 445—450.
6. Ibid., page 89, 235
7. Ibid., page 235—237, 445
8. Castells, M. (1976), Is there an Urban Sociology? In Pickvance, C., *Urban Sociology.* New York: St. Martin's Press, page 33—59.
9. Saunders, *Social Theory and the Urban Question*, op. cit.
10. Ibid.
11. For overviews of these discussions, see: Soja, E. (2000), *Postmetropolis*, Cambridge, Mass.: Blackwell.
12. Harvey, D. (1989), *The Urban Experience.* Baltimore: Johns Hopkins Press; and Harvey, D. (1982), *The Limits to Capital.* Chicago: University of Chicago Press.
13. Soja, E. (1989), *Postmodern Geographies.* New York: Verso, page 94—117.
14. Knox, P. L. and Taylor, P. J. (1995), *World Cities in a World-System*. New York: Cambridge University Press; and Scott, A. J. (1998), *Regions and the World Economy.* London: Oxford University Press; and Storper, M. (1998), *The Regional World.* New York: Guilford.
15. Graham, S. and Marvin, S. (2002), *Splintering Urbanism: Networked Infrastructures, Technological Nobilities and the Urban Condition.* New York: Routledge; and Taylor, P. J. (2004), *World City Network: A Global Urban Analysis.* New York: Routledge.
16. Brenner, N. (2004), *New State Spaces: Urban Governance and The Rescaling of Statehood.* New York: Oxford University Press; and Jessop, B. (2002), *The Future of the Capitalist State.* London: Polity.
17. Boyer, R. and Hollingsworth, J. R. (1997), From National Embeddedness to Spatial and Institutional Nestedness. In Boyer, R. and Hollingsworth, J. R., *Contemporary Capitalism: The Embeddedness of Institutions.* New York: Cambridge University Press, page 470—472
18. Swyngedouw, E., Neither Global nor Local: Glocalization and the Politics of Scale, op. cit.; and Brenner, N., *New State Spaces: Urban Governance and The Rescaling of Statehood*, op. cit.
19. Jessop, B., *The Future of the Capitalist State*, op. cit.
20. Sheppard, E. S. and McMaster, R. B. (2004), *Scale and Geographic Inquiry: Nature, Society, and Method.* Malden, Mass.: Blackwell.
21. Brenner, N. (2001), The Limits to Scale? Methodological Reflections on Scalar Structuration. In *Progress in Human Geography* 15 (4), page 525—548; and Marston, S. A., *The Social Construction of Scale*, op. cit.
22. Brenner, N. (2008), A Thousand Leaves: Notes on The Geographies of Uneven Spatial Development. In Keil, R. and Mahon, R., *A New Leviathan?*, Vancouver: University of British Columbia Press; and Jessop, B., Brenner, N. and Jones, M. (2008), Theorizing Sociospatial Relations In *Environment and Planning D.*
23. Brenner, N., The Limits to Scale? Methodological Reflections on Scalar Structuration, op. cit.
24. Brenner, N. and Theodore, N. (2003), *Spaces of Neoliberalism: Urban Restructuring in North America and Western Europe.* Cambridge, Mass.: Blackwell

Jacques Lévy, is a geographer and an urbanist. He is a full Professor at the EPFL. He is the director of the EPFL Chôros lab and co-director of the Collège des Humanités. He has been invited professor at various universities: UCLA NYU, USP (São Paulo), L'Orientale (Naples), Macquarie (Sydney), and the Reclus Chair in Mexico City. He has been fellow of the Wissenschaftskolleg zu Berlin. He has been invited as a keynote speaker to many congresses and conferences throughout the world. His major concerns are social theory of space, urbanity, globalization, cartography, spatial development, and the epistemology of social sciences. He has completed numerous research projects, including theoretical reflections and field studies on metropolises worldwide, and urban and territorial projects.

Public space in a global perspective: criteria and cultural dimensions. As you might

know, Monsieur Jourdain, a character of the French seventeenth-century writer Molière, is very happy to discover one day that he is able to speak in prose: he thought prose was as difficult as poetry, but with the help of a teacher he discovers that he can also speak in prose. In this respect, I would like to learn with you to "speak" public space, to rearrange what we know or what we think we know about cities, introducing this concept, which now seems obvious in sciences of the city but is nonetheless almost new.

It appeared roughly during the second half of the twentieth century: of course you have mentions of public space before, but something else was probably meant by this term. So, in trying to make this re-arrangement I think we have to follow the advice that Neil Brenner gave us, avoiding empiricism and positivism, and I would add some other elements that need to be avoided, such as anti-urban ideologies: there is a strong anti-urban current in the sciences of the city, which in a sense is strange, and, as I see it, there is a relationship between these anti-urban ideologies and the resistance of two epistemological and theoretical movements, or currents, which are economism and structuralism, which are related to each other. To explain what I mean I would say that my perspective lies in the theoretical context of a complex approach to the social world, which is to say that there is no hierarchical structure between economics and other social fields (which is the opposite of structuralism). This is very important, as Neil [Brenner] and Christian [Schmid] reminded us: there is an interesting and thought-provoking tradition that comes from Engels, who was the first to introduce this kind of theory, which is not the worst one. Because *The Condition of the Working Class in England* of the 1845, is really a very interesting text, better than many twentieth-century works on geography; however I would argue that, as Christian [Schmid] said, in this work, as in the works of the early Castells, like *The Urban Question*, cities are seen as effects and consequences of something else, which I would call economy, infrastructure, etc... So, there are certain views that divide empirical things and the hierarchies within a society into different boxes. The idea of the "material" being more important than the "immaterial", which Marx calls ideology or super-structure, I think it is not only related to Marxism, but linked to some other aspects in economic reductionism, which are very trendy indeed and actually the founding principle of economics. So I think that what we are addressing now is no weak adversary, saying that we should not use a hierarchical and causal model putting the economy first and the rest as secondary causes or mere effects; for instance, in

the urban field I would not say that peri-urbanisation
is mainly the result of economic forces, as we ordinar-
ily define them; I would say that peri-urbanisation is
the outcome of a certain model of society and being
together that refuses exposure to otherness, and that
prefers the privatization of daily life to exposure inside
public space.

If we want to explain peri-urbanisation or even subur-
banisation, as we saw it in America in the second half
of the twentieth century, it is more efficient to use ex-
planatory models other than economy-based ones. Of
course this can be discussed and always argued and,
as Neil Brenner explained, an invitation to reflexivity
is very important, but we have to practice reflexivity
on all the objects we use, for instance when we use
the word "capitalist" or "capitalism": it is not the same
to say that "there are capitalists" (first statement), "there
are capitalist logics or rationales" (second statement),
and that "we live inside capitalism" (third statement).
The three statements are different: I agree with the first
two, but not with the third one, because this is typically the result of the criticisms, ideas and ideologies,
saying that economics is hierarchically superior to
other disciplines in social theory. I tell you this because
you have to be very careful with what I am going to
tell you: all seems obvious but it is not. Behind what I
am saying there is a social theory that gives a role to
politics, a certain role to individuals, to organizations,
to the environment. So, don't naively believe what I am
telling you!

Ideas about the future of cities and public space. I won't try
to demonstrate anything, but I would like to be clear,
as Peter Sloterdijk says about science, that our work is
mainly about explicitation; of course it is not enough,
because we must not neglect empirical work (we are
paid for this!) but on the theoretical side explicitation
is a very important part of our job. So, to begin with,

	Co-presence	Mobility	Tele-communication
Accessibility to indentified information	−	=	+
Serendipity	+	=	−
Exposure to place otherness	−	+	−
Exposure to body otherness	+	=	−
Type of space generated	Place, territory	Territory, network	Network, place
Examples	City, family	Intercity and intracity transportation networks	Mail, books, the Web

Public space and the comparative advantage of urban choice.
courtesy of Jacques Levy

fig. 9

I would like to make some observations on the context we are facing: first, we are experiencing the end of absolute urbanisation; Christian Schmid explained it in reference to Switzerland, and Switzerland is of course part of the world. So, what is true for Switzerland is true for the rest of the world: the stock of rural population is limited, and people who can be put into the "urban" have historical limits, because the overall population of the world is in a sense a limited stock. We have to imagine a totally urbanized world with internal rearrangements that we can call "relative urbanisation processes", identified by Christian [Schmid] at the end of his presentation (☞ page 68, Christian Schmid), but these are rearrangements inside the same envelope, which is a completely urbanized world. It is important to keep this in mind, because it means that when we

consider urban processes, or explicit massive voluntary urban processes, like urbanism, what we once called "urban planning" (which I now prefer to call "urbanism"), we have to keep in mind how today it is something other than what it used to be for example in 1950s Europe, when the goal was to arrange fluxes, flows of absolute urbanisation and to build shelters and services for newcomers in the urban world. Now the point is different, for it involves reorganizing an already urbanized population, the already urbanized areas and spatial configurations. The second thing I would like to point out is that in recent decades urban areas have demonstrated their capability to cope with the challenges of development. You remember that in the 1960s Melvin Webber prophesized a world where cities wouldn't be useful anymore—what he called "no place". A world where differentiation between places in terms of concentration wouldn't be relevant anymore: he thought this because private mobility would be the main solution to the problem of distance management. Co-presence is a way of dealing with mobility, the utopia of the zero-dimensional space. Mobility instead is an alternative solution; so Melvin Webber thought, seeing the development of what was called at that time the Los Angeles model— as Christian [Schmid] reminded us—that this could work in the future; the fact that Los Angeles would create subways was just impossible to imagine. Quite the contrary, the idea was that cities with an underground system would abandon it to live in the suburbs with private houses and private cars. And this was of course an important trend at the end of the twentieth century, and it still is a trend, but with historical experience we can see that we are not experiencing the end of cities. Another model proposing the end of cities in the near future was that of William Mitchell in the 1990s: you will have heard about *City of Bits*, a small but clever book which replaces all the spatial expressions linked to the city with metaphorical expressions related to the Internet and cyberspace. So, Mitchell's argument was to say that we will have virtual cities and space, and that we don't need physical cities anymore. I think he was wrong and he himself recognized this in his later books, in which there is a much more qualified approach to the relationship between cities and cyberspace.

So, in this table I would like to express the simple idea that spatial concentration, the co-presence of the maximum of social life in the minimum extension (in big and small spaces as well) possesses some comparative advantages, particularly in a society which gives value to creativity and the kind of production which cannot be planned: the sciences are typically not planned and serendipity is typically a productive force. In this kind of productive context cities have real advantages and what I am trying to say in this presentation is that there is a relationship between serendipity and body-otherness, because the fact that in a public space you put your body in danger, at the risk of others' action, has very important political consequences. It creates a

Jacques Lévy

certain social body, but it also has cognitive consequences, which are encompassed by the fact that our body has multi-sensoriality, and insofar as the Internet is concerned it is quite easy to have the benefits of transmission of acoustic and visual messages but it is not so easy for the other senses, and probably it won't be in the near future. What is interesting about multi-sensoriality is that it is also a mix of senses, a kind of impression that you can't reduce to the sum of different uni-sensorial perceptions, but a complex combination of all perceptions. We can discuss this table and compare its pluses and minuses but the fundamental thesis is that cities have important comparative advantages in this emerging creative society. But what do we mean by "public space" in this context?

Conditions for public space. It is important for us to distinguish public space from apparently similar spaces: a public space for instance is not the public domain, nor open state-ruled property. There might be private property which is public space, because the rules of public space are implemented in it. It is not also the public scene: we incur now into an epistemological problem about translation, because particularly in English and French many people translate "Öffentlichkeit" as "public space", but for me it would be something like the "public realm": everything that is public. In terms of public space we actually intend "space" as a metaphor. And here there is a problem because space is not only a metaphor, and so I would say, with Hannah Arendt, Jürgen Habermas and Kant, that public space is actually an aspect of the public realm, because in public space we have public goods. But the public goods does not mean collective goods: in English the pervasive use of the term "community" is a problem for social sciences. Society, for instance, is not collective but it also includes collectivity, objects, organizations, memory, identity, environments… So,

	Amsterdam	Johannerburg
Density	+	–
Compactness	+	–
Cross-accessibility of urban places	+	–
Public space	+	–
Pedestrian (=public) metrics	+	–
Co-presence dwelling/jobs	+	–
Diversity of activities	+	–
Sociological mix	+	–
Intra-urban polarities	+	–
Per capita productivity	+	–
Positive self-valuation of all urban places	+	–
Presevation of natural environment (soil, water, air)	+	–
Self-visibility and self-identification of the urban society	+	–
Urban-scale polity	+	–

In a fully urbanized world, urbanity models are society models.
courtesy of Jacques Levy

fig. 10

society is a system and reducing it to a collectivity of human beings is not an efficient way of defining it, and when you define a public good as a type of good which is produced by society as a whole and whose benefits are given to society as a whole, it means that this is not directly linked to a group of people. That's why I distinguish public from common goods (a trendy new concept with the latest Nobel Prize for Economics). What is interesting in a public space (and even makes it utopian) is that it does not belong to a group, as I was saying, but to nobody, to society. Public space is one of the critical indicators of a society's capability to represent itself, because in a public space you can't ignore the question: "where am I now?". Is it an environment designed by others but I have the right to experience it, and it could be something that I can change through my own action. Its particular situation changes the nature of the place. Public space is a place where you could expect to experience a level of urban diversity whose magnitude might be similar to that of the overall urban area. At least two scales (neighborhood, city country, continent, world…) are therefore always necessary when addressing a public space: the scale of the place itself and that of its reference area. You can't address a public space if you define it in terms of diversity without defining the content of this diversity, and this is given by a second scale: a global city, a metropolis, takes the world as its main reference; if we want to understand and to decide whether or not we are facing a public space, this is a question that regards scale. Also, we have both fixed and mobile public space: we can define public mobility as the mobility that requires public space. So, in this technical system of movement we have mobile public space, like vehicles, trains, trams, and so on but also tools, switchers between mobility and immobility; in this context we can define public metrics as the set of relationships

04 h 40 min

to distance and mobility that possess a public dimension and that constitute mobility as a public good. For example, personal mobility has no particular causal relationship with private mobility, and indeed maybe it's the opposite, personal mobility is therefore, logically, public mobility (but not collective). Car-pooling and car-sharing, by the way, are both individual and public.

Degrees of public space. I'd like to show the strong relationship between public space and the issues about the city that are at stake now in almost all cities throughout the world: the first issue is a historical hesitation between two models of urbanity, which are also models of societies, here represented by Amsterdam and Johannesburg in the table. The self-visibility of society is very important in public space, a very concrete and tangible expression of diversity: it is not sufficient to say that Los Angeles is a lively mix of Blacks, Mexicans, Chicanos etc... and then go out only to a tennis beach on Sundays and see only people like yourself in Santa Monica. For my observations and readings I am interested in these issues, discussed not only by urbanists and politicians, but also by ordinary dwellers who buy their options and choose. Of course they don't all have the same level of choice but as far as they can they choose to follow one model or the other. The Amsterdam model is to be found more in city centers in Europe and Asia, and the Johannesburg model in suburbia and North America.
But the picture which emerged in the 1980s has been modified by what is generally called ecological awareness: valuing proximity and the "Heideggerian" on one hand, and on the other the right to mobility and even an injunction to mobility, arouses awareness that the environment is a problem to be addressed, and we have to communicate and meet in order to create a political society that can manage and handle

Jacques Lévy

(☞ fig. 10)

these huge global problems. So, depending on which model of society you choose, you will have completely different approaches to space in general and to cities in particular; it is clear that urbanity, which deals with a completely man-made environment, is not very popular nowadays. Here again you have a clear relation between the big issues that are at stake in our urban society and public space. One example is that you can have green cars that would satisfy the natural environment but not so easily satisfy social cohesion. It's not enough to change car engines, because the fact that you have private or public mobility changes the conditions of social life considerably.

In conclusion, I would say that public space is at stake at any scale: of course it is at stake at small scales, but, as I've tried to show, it is also at stake on larger scales for two reasons: first, because there is a need to comprehend public spaces at higher scales and, secondly, because urban humanity is discussing the role of urban space; it is global for two converging but different reasons. I am struck by the fact that I am tempted to consider that there is a singular historical parallelism between singular historical cities throughout the world; of course this is not a simple evolutionary model, but it takes into account the fact that something can be invented two or three times without sufficient levels of communication and, on the other side, the fact that there is a certain capacity of accumulation in human history, so a part of humanity could be replicated by others. I believe that every metropolis has introduced a pro-car and anti-urban policy, but almost all cities are now switching to a more pro-urbanity policy. What is interesting and gives value to my point is that if you look at China nowadays you find all three stages of urbanisation simultaneously. For instance, from the destruction in Shanghai of a motorway viaduct in view of the Expo, built only two decades ago, we find now a linear public space: China,

(☞ fig. 11)

	Stage 1	Stage 2	Stage 3
Definition of the Stage Asian Metropolises	Anti-urbanity urbanisation policy Tokyo, 1950-70s; Hong Kong, 1970-80s; Bangkok, 1980-90s	Dual, ambivalent urbanisation policy Bangkok, Djakarta, Manila, Delhi, Mumbai, Chennai, Kolkata, today	Pro-urbanity urbanisation policy Tokyo, Osaka, Singapore, Seoul, Taipei, taday
West European and North American Metropolises	Western Europe, 1950-70s; North America, 1930-90s	Western Europe, 1980-90s; North America, today	Western Europe, today

Urbanisation and the public space: three stages.
courtesy of Jacques Levy

fig. 11

a very big industrial country with specific relationships between industry and cities, is sometimes avant-garde in terms of its post-industrial, pro-urbanity policies. So, my real conclusion is that public space has become a continuous global archipelago and a key issue for the globalized urban world. As an indicator of urban globalization (or global urbanisation) we could use this emerging continuity between all public spaces, both mobile and fixed, as if it were the main web of global civic societies. This is quite understandable if you take into account pedestrian spaces, trams, subways, underground, but what about airplanes? Is the airplane a part of the global continuity of public space? I think it is a good issue both for practical and theoretical fields, because the specificity of the plane is that for long distances you don't have any alternative; those who have the opportunity to use a car can't use it for long distances. They are forced to stay with other very different people, and in planes we can observe all the endeavors of these people who refuse exposure to otherness to avoid contacts with people "below" them.

Theses on urban / public space. Elaborating on the prevously advanced ideas about the future of cities and public space, Jacques Lévy with Véronique Mauron, Monique Ruzicka Rossier, and Gian Paolo Torricelli suggest fifteen theses, concerning public space, to be submitted to the open debate.

1. The existence of public space in a specific area of the planet cannot be taken for granted.
The presence of public space is not equally distributed in different societies. Anti-historical culturalist approaches assume that all societies possess the same quantity of public space, but express them in different ways. Quite to the contrary, it can be argued that the possibility of having public space is strictly dependent on certain fundamental characteristics of a society. In Gemeinschaft-based social configurations, rural societies or societies organised upon a principle of strict segregation, public spaces cannot be observed. Conversely, the presence of public space can be linked to the strength of an individual-centered model of society, as Norbert Elias has coined it, even if this strength is only a work in progress or a slowly emerging process.

2. Designing a public space is neither necessary nor sufficient, but it can be extremely useful, if the designer accepts not to be the only actor in the process. A public space cannot be decreed but only observed *post aut propter*. Public space does not always and obviously appear where one expects it to. If within Western societies, public space mainly emerges in streets, public squares, parks and transport connexions, it also extends itself beyond these territories, becoming a profusion and braking out of its traditional boundaries. Public space is of an unstable, floating nature, generating an inner movement that makes it migrate, or shift from one place to another. This phenomenon is described as 'society taking a walk'. In this context, another idea can be put forward: public space is not always manifested where public authorities had planned it to be, nor where architects had designed it to be. It can arise outside of the range of action of these space-arranging authorities, and outside of planned infrastructures. As a consequence, the urbanist's role can be defined as that of a supporter to the public space production process; guiding, among others, an initiative that enables action to unfold itself within a given territory. The urban designer does not create public space—only the will and desires of individuals to mix, and to encounter each other are public space's true makers. Public space bears a metric—it can be observed, examined, measured, and outlined on maps and projects... and yet, at the same time, it is an open relational space, both immaterial and not easily measurable. Amidst some cities, public space tends to regenerate itself without requiring the matrix of physical—that is to say, 'architectural'—realities, and does so using solely the agency of interpersonal interactions, of various types of solidarity and coexistence at various scales. Public space then becomes a self-made and self-managed component of a local spatial identity. The informal production of public space should therefore be taken in consideration. Urban design is not an answer but a question. Architects and urban planners are important actors in a public space, but by no means the only ones. Urbanism is a matter of experts, social stakeholders and, above all, ordinary citizens. When an urbanist designs a potential space he asks urban society a question: would you accept transforming this virtual public space in an actual one? Actors of this society will have the last word.

3. A public space is a public good. A public good is a social good that is, at least partially, consumed—and often produced—by the society at large. The notion of public good is often mentioned at the World scale, but it makes sense, too, at the city scale. It is in such a way that public space must be thought of as a public good—involving a portion which is immediate, free cost, tacitly produced by all, and available for all. Public space understood as a public good shared by all actors concerned transforms each and every one of them into one another's equal. In such a way, public space must be considered as a universal right acquired through urbanity. The public world is not a collective entity: it is homologous to society as a whole, including its non-human components (objects, environments). Conversely, when a space pertains to a specific group, it loses its public nature.

4. Public space builds itself upon the weak ties shared by those who embody it. The substance of 'public space' as a public good is based upon the existence and preservation of weak ties. When individuals attempt to transform these weak ties into strong ties—whether it be through private interpersonal bonds, residency, or the segregation of some part of social otherness—the public nature of a space tends to be threatened. Any privatisation imposed by an individual or collective dweller constitutes a breach to the tacit social contract, according to which the inhabitants of a city who forge its public space through their interactions accept a self-limitation of their relations to weak-tie types.

5. Public space represents. Public space gathers, on the one hand, the general perceptions relative to a city that have been established and organised throughout various narratives, statements, or maps, and on the other hand, the mental perceptions, images and symbols produced and experienced by every urban actor through the help of his interpretation and imagination. Referring to Henri Lefebvre's theory, public space is both a perception one has of space, and a space within which one can be perceived. That space enables stakeholders at large—whether they be permanent dwellers, tourists, or one of the different powers in place—to see each other. It offers a visibility to society at large. It is a common image that provides a meaning to the acceptance of differences.

6. The pedestrian constitutes public space's fundamental metric. Public space's main qualities are to be measured in terms of availability (degree of exposure) and diversity (degree of otherness). The pedestrian is an inhabitant and incarnation that both produces public space's proper dimensions and takes advantage of it. Public space is intended in the first place for that particular actor. The pedestrian can be seen as the central figure within public spatial practice. Synaesthesia, and the serendipity that comes with it are powerful cognitive tools that make public space a critical device for an innovation and creation-oriented society. So far, other mechanisms that allow for random exposure to new information, like the Web, have not attained the same degree of efficiency. Public space takes place in at the very core of cities' comparative advantage among spatial configurations.

7. Public spaces can be either fixed or mobile. A significant part of existing public spaces are directly or indirectly mobile. Public vehicles (trains, trams, buses,...) as well as stations, bus stops, or other 'airlocks' between urban territory and transportation networks are public spaces structurally defined by their contribution to the mobility system. Even traditional fixed public spaces like streets or squares are profoundly shaped by mobility. A permanent stay in a public space is a first step towards privatisation. The pedestrian extends his spatiality within the public transportation system. As a matter of fact, the latter, contrarily to a car for example, maintains high levels of otherness, anonymity, and of availability. Public transportation does not separate the individual from his urban environment: it maintains the same degree of urbanity as when he is a pedestrian. Through such a process, public mobility both consumes and produces public space. We thus state that the pedestrian, through different means of transportation—individual and public transportation—engenders public space. The combination of fixed and mobile public spaces not only creates a continuous territory at the city scale, but far beyond it, too. It can be argued that the worldwide archipelago of public spaces is becoming the elementary web for an emerging global civil society, and as a result, one of the fundamental base-maps of the contemporary World.

8. Civility is public space's typical political expression. Within public space, a societal model is generated that cannot be reduced to institutional democracy, for it is subject to a multiple individual responsibilities towards public goods. One of the major consequences emanating from such a conception of public space as a public good is that public space produces civil society. Public space is not just an expression of civil society: it is an 'actant', capable of operating upon it and transforming it. In other words we can say that public space manufactures a certain type of political force: civility. Civility reinvents, by its own means and through the instrument of every interaction, politics as the action of being together. Nevertheless, public space as a public good needs to obtain its legitimacy through political action and thus requires an intentional determination. Such an expression must not restrict itself simply to infrastructure, but must bear an 'order of civilities', composed of mental realities, not to say rules and laws, that determine interactions and practices. When dealing with public space, one cannot distinguish the *urbs* from the *civitas*. A 'cityness' including the practice of public space cannot thus be observed without some kind of citizenship.

9. Public space does not limit itself to the public arena. The notion of public space as we understand it does not entirely fit that of the public sphere (Öffentlichkeit) as Jürgen Habermas has defined it. Space's 'public' feature emerges because political action starts flowing within it. It is by the hand of civility that public space binds itself to the public sphere. Civility is politics without polity. If one reduces the public sphere to the agora's deliberation arena, then public space does not participate in its constitution. However, public spaces can contribute to political pluralist debate through some specific events, like outdoor rallies or street demonstrations. Conversely, a space arranged as an incarnation of power in action, especially throughout its particular scale or its particular geometry, outlines the rejection of individual dwellers from the production process of that space's qualities. If such an attempt succeeds, that space is deprived of its public feature. Moreover, the public sphere is often seen as the 'public domain', or the 'state property' notion. Nevertheless, no connection can be made between a land's ownership and the public feature of the space relative to it. A street is not necessarily a public space; the interior space of a private bus company is a sort of public space. In a nutshell, public space is a specific component of the public sphere, which must be distinguished both from the public arena and from state property.

10. Through the exposure of his very body the inhabitant transforms public space into a political environment. Within a public space, the absence of violence is due to the fact that each and everyone's fragile being is placed under the protection of all. If a society's traditional victims of domination and violence—women, children, outsiders, etc...—cannot reside in a space then this space should not be considered 'public'. Public space generates both anonymous encounters and local pacification. Compared to other important distance management methods—such as mobility or tele-communication—public space possesses a specificity. Within this specificity, a co-presence can be observed that implies a bodily involvement that, on the one hand, puts its owner at risk, but on the other hand, simultaneously ensures the existence of a being-together. It is because of such an implication that public space's contribution to the constitution of a political society appears so essential.

11. Public space protects and reinforces intimacy. Intimacy / extimacy is a different dyad from the classical private / public opposition. The engaged and exhibited presence of one's body appearing in a public space implies the fact that even if what is public is an antonym to privacy, it is nevertheless not the rejection of intimacy at all. On the contrary, intimacy turns out to be far better protected within public space than in the various private locations where the individual can end up harmed by an undesired group. Amidst public space, the individual, on his own or within an interaction, develops specific experiences that pertain both to an intimate domain and to the unfolding of one's personality, while compatible with the restrictions implied by civility.

12. Public space spreads out onto several gradients. Pure public space is a utopia, an ideal whose perceivable and tangible materialisations are imperfect and fragile standards. In order to exist, however, public space does not need the complete expression of all of its constituting elements (availability, diversity, interaction, various types of flow, anonymity, civility, appropriation, memory, and readability). Public space is unstable and submitted to alterations. Consequently, it is a variable space that cannot be described absolutely but only in relative terms, using gradients as a means to do so. Furthermore, public spaces are made up of a large array of complex phenomena, like fleeting, improvised, seasonal, and sometimes hardly perceivable performances or events. That is why the task of both adjusting and putting into balance those contradictory processes is necessary to define the level of publicity a given public space contains. Measuring public space requires scrollbar-like indicators in motion, which will make manifest a continuum of gradients. Thus approached, public space turns out to be an efficient benchmarking instrument for a city's vitality.

13. Any public space implies at least two scales. A public space cannot be analysed without taking into account at least two scales: its own and that of its referential societal space. The latter defines the degree of diversity the public space reproduces within it, which can be multiple: a city, a region, a country, a continent, or the World. Since centuries ago, various metropolises which became imperial

Jacques Lévy, Véronique Mauron, Monique Ruzicka Rossier, Gian Paolo Torricelli

capitals have amassed a diversity of world-scale social realities. The current globalization process enables every city to increase its referential space to that of the World. Through its either temporary or permanent inhabitants, cultural or economic activities, and architectural styles and ways of life, public space has come to offer a wide range of rich, unique, world-scale collections of social realities.

14. A public space is open to changes in its norms and its uses, carried out by those who inhabit it. Those changes can either enhance or undermine its public nature. The content of a public space is, by construction, made up of the sum and combination of interactions carried out within it. This means that there is no permanence in the concrete actualisation of its characteristics. The definition of what is useful, pleasant, allowed, and appropriate in a public space is the instantaneous outcome of the permanent 'discussion' carried out by the actors that make this space public. The total institutionalisation of a public space (for instance by a tight police control in the street or in shopping malls) will undermine the public nature of a space, as well as privatisation processes (for example the establishment of a stable residential shelter). The invention and implementation of unplanned activities are, conversely, positive because they increase the level of diversity, on the condition that the level of accessibility is at least maintained. Micro-events or minor alterations can have significant short-term and long-term impact on the very nature of the place. This shows the delicate and fragile nature of a public space, which can conserve and express the memory of happy or traumatic experiences.

15. Public space is par excellence a generator and an indicator of urbanity. Public space is the art of being in town and of living in town. It shapes every dweller's urbanity, whose gestures, speeches and actions provide public space with its own 'advertisement'. Circulation within public spaces prepares people to be 'augmented' individuals through the experience of city life. Reciprocally, such an art—in the sense of both a 'savoir-faire' and a 'savoir-être'—encourages public space in its public nature. The urban actor who develops a practical understanding of public space knows what he can make of the city. Public space encounters its utmost conditions for emergence in large cities. Nevertheless, in the same way as can be observed in a generalised approach to urbanity, public space may reach an important degree of development within smaller urban areas, on the condition that both the diversity and accessibility levels are defined at the highest possible scale. Public space is therefore a good indicator of the gradient of urbanity achieved in an urban area. It is a driving force, too, and a momentum in the process of urbanity-making. As a result, it makes sense that the right to public space—if a society decides to declare it—is virtually an equivalent proposition to that of the right to the city.

GLOBALIZATION OF URBANITY

Summer School
USUM abstracts

research abstract

Christian Schmid, ☞ page 50.

Tracing global urbanisation. Starting

from Henri Lefebvre's famous thesis of the complete urbanisation of society, this contribution explores the main elements of contemporary urbanisation on a global scale. The problem faced today is that cities no longer constitute units that can be delimited; they are highly dynamic, multifaceted, and complex. A dual approach is required in order to grasp these factors: On the one hand, a "horizontal", synchronical analysis is needed that starts from the current situation of the territory, determines the expansion and interweaving of urban regions, and reveals variations in the processes of urbanisation. On the other, urban development has to be understood and conceived as a historical production process. This requires a historical, "vertical", diachronical analysis. The horizontal analysis is dedicated to the patterns of urbanisation as they currently present themselves. While increasingly exact data and detailed methods are available today to analyze the structure of a city, experience has shown that, in most cases, precise mapping of spatial phenomena can only create the appearance of exactness. Urbanisation is a complex process that is constantly changing shape. Therefore, no given representation can deliver more than just a snapshot. Furthermore, urban reality comprises very diverse attributes that are superimposed as stratified layers. Accordingly, many different lines of demarcation can be drawn, depending on the observer's perspective and heuristic interest. On the base of the horizontal analysis, a vertical, historical analysis of the pathways of urbanisation should follow. It descends into the past to identify the defining moments that have inscribed themselves into the terrain and the collective memory. Subsequently, the analysis must ascend again in order to attempt to reconstruct the decisive lines of development and to elaborate a timeline oriented along the respective dominant constellations of power and the most important fields of conflict. In particular, it is crucial to identify the constants and the discontinuities in the development. This analysis does not simply aim at reconstructing the history of a city, but wants to detect the ways in which history remains present in the contemporary situation and influences the future trajectory.

Pascal Kallenberger, born in 1981 in Zurich,

studied Urban Geography, National Economics, and Planning at the University of Zurich, ETH Zurich, and at the University of Sheffield. Currently, he is doing his PhD at the ETH Zurich and is working with Prof. Christian Schmid as a research assistant on the USUM— Urban Systems and Urban Models project. He is a member of the INURA—International Network for Urban Research and Action. He is particularly interested in urban and planning theory, the history of ideas, and environmental planning.

+

Monika Streule, born in 1977 in Zurich, studied

Cultural Anthropology, Sociology and International Relations at the University of Zurich. She lived and worked in Mexico City for research on an ongoing project of restructuring the Mexican historic center and the social impact of such global processes of urban transformation. Concepts such as space, power and identity are crucial in her research. Currently, she is working with Prof. Christian Schmid as a research assistant on the USUM—Urban Systems and Urban Models project on patterns and pathways of global urbanisation processes. In particular, she is interested in urban anthropology, urban social movements, qualitative social research, and an actor-centered approach. She works on issues concerning the constitution of urban spaces and everyday practices of appropriation of public spaces.

Urbanisation processes: comparing Kolkata and Mexico City.

In this presentation the first results of the ongoing research project on urbanisation processes in Mexico City and Kolkata will be presented. After a short introduction to the urban development of both cases, the main focus will be on the patterns and pathways of urbanisation in these cities. The aim is to present the current findings and the applied method of analysis in these two specific cities in order to discuss further possible steps towards a comparative approach. The presentation will start with a discussion of the urban patterns (horizontal analysis) of Mexico City and Kolkata and the mapping work done so far. In a second step, the dependence on history and urban development will be explained (vertical analysis). It will be argued that to understand urbanisation processes both perspectives are crucial. In a more detailed analysis, two case studies will be presented: Ciudad Nezahualcóyotl in Mexico City, and Howrah in Kolkata, both representing very particular urban configurations with a very strong informal component.

research abstract

Jorge Peña Díaz, is the former Head of the Centre for Urban Studies of Havana and is currently the Dean of the Faculty of Architecture. He has developed his career from the Faculty of Architecture of Havana through his scientific research and professional practice as an architect. The main aspects of his scientific career at the Centre for Urban Studies of Havana are those of urban analysis, urbanism, landscape architecture and planning and sustainable strategies and environment-oriented projects. He has also worked on projects related to the use of CAD systems as supporting tools for urban planning and design. In collaboration with partners from other fields, he has participated in artistic exhibition projects linked to his research and practice activities. An important part of his career is connected to his academic activities as a design studio leader at the Faculty of Architecture. He has joined teaching activities and research projects with colleagues from several foreign universities, including University of Brighton, TU-Dortmund, Technical University of Managua, ETH Zurich, and EPFL.

Havana: Slow Motion Urbanism. The

presentation presents the exceptional case of Havana. This situation appears when contrasting the urbanisation process that has taken place there during the past half century against the background of accelerated contemporary global urbanisation. The process of urbanisation on the global scale—along with the overflowing of urban landscapes and the emergence of megacities—seems to be bypassing Havana. The current urban situation is depicted and three main driving forces of the process are presented: the blockade, the impact of the economic crisis of the past two decades, and local urban policies.

research abstract

Rolf Jenni, completed his education in Architecture at the technical high school in 1994, followed by studies in Architecture at the University of Applied Sciences in Biel from 1993 to 1997. From 2004 to 2006 he expanded his education with a postgraduate study in Architecture and Urbanism at the Berlage Institute in Rotterdam. He has taught in design studios at the ETH Zurich and at the University of Applied Science FHNW in Basel as a teaching assistant and has been engaged in the ETH Studio Basel since 2007, as a researcher and teaching assistant. He has lectured and has been a guest critic at various universities, including the ETH Zurich, TU Delft, the Berlage Institute and the TU in Munich. In addition to teaching and academia, he has been collaborating with various architectural firms in Switzerland and Holland since 1997. In 2007, together with Tom Weiss, he established Raumbureau, an architecture and urbanism office in Zurich.

Hong Kong: State Entrepreneurial Urbanism.

Hong Kong had developed in just fifty years from a colonial city known for its spontaneous and informal urban growth to a highly controlled and formalised urbanisation model, simultaneously and continuously involving neo-liberal strategies. This coupling of liberalism and control might at first glance seem contradictory, since capitalist liberalism is very often associated with a 'laissez-faire' attitude, but in the case of Hong Kong, "control and laissez-faire" eventually became an economically successful strategy for the post-colonial government. This lecture sketches out an understanding of the specific characteristics of the entrepreneurial governing model, striving for maximum efficiency and perfection, while trying to explore its complex mechanisms and the roles of its various actors. The complex mechanisms at play are revealed by an investigation into the public transport and infrastructure system of HK, which functions as a link between the HKSAR Government and the ostensibly private transportation company to generate profit through real-estate developments. As its main aim, the lecture will try to construct the argument that the direct relationship between transport infrastructure and property development led to the infrastructure node, a new and highly profitable urban typology. This node-network-system and its corresponding typology may serve the government today as the ultimate instrument to generate high land value through accessibility and high density of vertically organised programs. The typological architectural features that the steadily developed economic and urban model involves are analyzed through the project for Lohas Park, a version of the latest station—or node-type currently under construction which can be regarded as the ultimate embodiment of this typology and urban development.

research abstract

Jacques Levy, ☞ page 94.

Definitions and theses on globalization and urban / public space.

The presentation chooses to define public space as follows: Public space is: (1) The city's space that offers free access, with configurations and limits proper to it; (2) A public environment—a relational space formed by the interactions occurring within it. Public space is the individual being confronted by society; (3) A portion of societal space within which any actor taking part expects to experience an equivalent amount of diversity to that encountered within that portion's referential space; (4) A concentration of urbanity—public space makes the city to appear. Such definition transcends the traditional dualism encountered within the confrontation of the notions of Public Space and Public Realm—Public Space being the physical extension of a non-built architectural space that can be both measured and outlined on various maps, and the Public Realm being the sector pertaining to the city's various types of inhabitants. Public space is often a space that has been designed to enable public access. But it is above all a relational space—a place with the potential for meeting and exchange, and that can genuinely be accessed and utilized by everybody. If the latter characteristic is missing, one cannot assume one is observing an effective public space, but solely a virtual public space. On the other hand, it is possible to come across a public space that has not been designed but that effectively exists and is of satisfactory use for those who come upon it. Basing our reflection on such a definition, the presentation finally refers to the USUM WP3 fifteen theses (☞ page 108, Jacques Levy, Véronique Mauron, Monique Ruzicka Rossier, Gian Paolo Torricelli) concerning public space which have been submitted for debate between researchers of the various USUM WPs.

research abstract

Véronique Mauron, is a scientific collaborator at the EPFL Chôros lab. She has conducted scientific research on interdisciplinary anthropological questions about mourning, idiocy and reproductive medicine. She is currently researching Public Space and teaching Space in Contemporary Art at EPFL.

Tools for a globalization and urban / public space research.

The USUM WP3 research is an observation and analysis of expressions of public space visible today in cities around the world. It focuses on the actors, practices, functions, objects, and shapes that constitute public space. This questions the universality of public space. The presentation gives a definition of public space. This definition highlights four aspects: (1) Public space offering free access, with configurations and limits proper to it; (2) The public environment—a relational space established by the interactions occurring within it. Public space is the individual being confronted by society; (3) A portion of societal space within which any actor taking part expects to experience an equivalent amount of diversity to that encountered within that portion's referential space; (4) A concentration of urbanity—public space makes the city appear. To make a comparative analysis of public spaces in cities around the world, USUM WP3 has developed several tools. These tools are both scientific objects and media that give visibility to the research: (a) Grid; Construction of an observation checklist to describe a public space qualitatively and schematically, this matrix collects the parameters needed for the production of public space; (b) Encyclopedia of public space: e-public-space.net; Creating an interactive encyclopedia in the form of a website which brings together many different documents (texts, images, sounds) dealing with public space in the world.

research abstract

Gian Paolo Torricelli, currently teaches Urban Geography at the Accademia di architettura in Mendrisio, where he is responsible for the Spatial Development Observatory, a small laboratory for monitoring and controlling the implementation of the Master Plan of Canton Ticino. He joined the USUM—Urban Systems and Urban Models coordinated research, collaborating with the EPFL Chôros lab on Public Space. He is a scientific advisor to the organization on issues of territory, and has taught at the universities of Geneva, Buenos Aires, Grenoble, and Milan.

Public space and power: can the African city learn from the Latin American urban experience? Comparing Bamako, Buenos Aires and Bogotá.

In the estimate of the UN agency Habitat, sub-Saharan African cities today consist of two thirds informal urbanisation sectors, practically slums without infrastructures, and without public equipment, where 165 million inhabitants are believed to live. According to the same source, the inhabitants of all African cities will increase from 350 million in 2005 to 1.2 billion in 2050. African and especially sub-Saharan cities—in the coming decades—will be the fastest growing cities in the world. Urban public space represents a very important part, where "spontaneous" urbanisation will continue to represent a great part of the building space for housing. In this context of a huge population increase, this means a high increase in the scarcity of land and a lack of available land for infrastructure and public spaces. In an age of globalization, what might the sub-Saharan city learn from recent Latin American urban experiences? The intention is to compare and to comment on some case-studies involving the production of city space. The experience in Bamako, among other things, concerns two situations that involve the urban public space as an element of power and at the same time two problematic situations for the future development of the city: (1) the gradual atrophy of public space (disappearing squares, playing fields, and parks) in poor residential areas, because of a great increase in competition between the families for urban land, linked to the phenomenon of corruption in the municipalities; (2) the total lack of mass public transport infrastructure and networks that can effectively connect the various areas of the city. We here point to two possible good practices that make it possible to expand public space in terms of the quality of life in a slum context, and urban public mobility. In the first case the production of urban space will be discussed from the point of view of the informal production of city space, the "Villa de Retiro" case in Buenos Aires (☞ page 129, Bruno Salerno). In the second case we will briefly discuss the development of the mass urban public transport system in Bogotá, which could potentially be adapted to the African city.

research abstract

Bruno Salerno, is a PhD candidate in Geography at the UBA—Universidad de Buenos Aires. He is PhD Scholar at the CONICET—Consejo Nacional de Investigaciones Científicas y Técnicas since 2010. He has got a PGTI09 Scholarship after having obtained a Geography degree in 2010 at the UBA in the Facultad de Filosofía y Letras with a thesis titled "Vivir sobre las vías del tren. La producción del espacio villero en la Ciudad Autónoma de Buenos Aires y el caso de la Toma de la manzana 106" supervised by Dr. Alejandro Benedetti.

"Espacio Villero" in Buenos Aires.

Traditionally, the production of the space of informal settlements in Buenos Aires has been related to individual and time-deferred practices. In recent decades, though, land seizure has become important for the production of the Villas. For our case of study, some traces of territoriality have been found to be involved in this mechanism. The case of study is the Villa de Retiro, and in particular one *manzana*—city block—at number 106, produced from an illegal land seizure in which the social movement Barrios de Pie took part as the organizers. The analysis of this movement's organizational logic and the way it operates in the Villa allow us to link its territoriality to concepts of barrio and public space. These categories appear as necessary elements that may be useful when considering the production of Villas in Buenos Aires during the past decade.

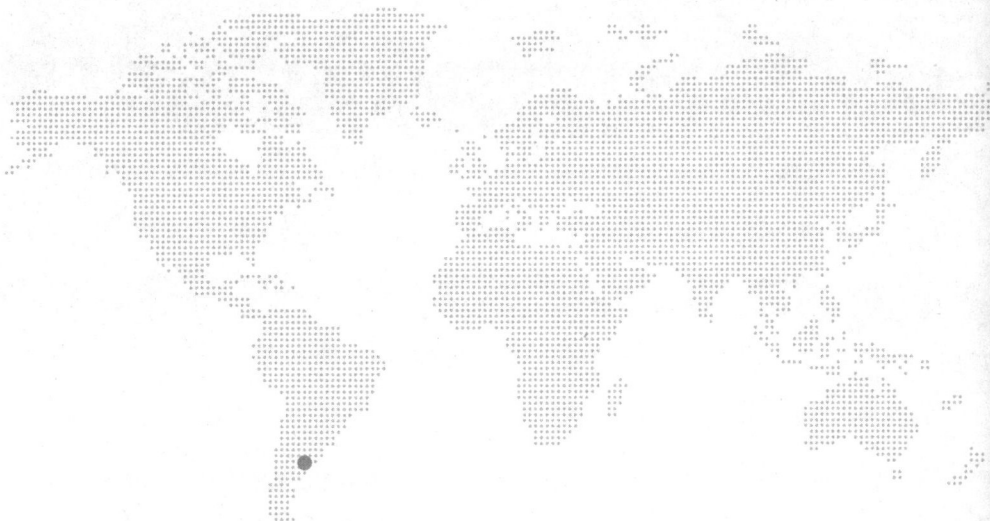

Beatrice Ferrari, received a Master's degree in
Geography and Anthropology from the University of Neuchâtel
and a Certificate of Chinese language from the Beijing University of
Language and Culture. She is currently a PhD candidate at Chôros
Lab, at the EPFL, where she also teaches Urban Planning and Urban
Culture in China. The research topics she is interested in include the
transformation of built environments, the production of cosmopolitan
spaces and the relationship between urbanisation and globalization
processes, with a particular focus on China. The objective of her PhD
research project is to better understand the approach of innovative
people in Beijing to the city and how they are contributing to its
inclusion in worldwide networks.

Public space in Beijing.

Public space in Beijing. The presentation is a short exploration of public space in Beijing (and elsewhere). But how do we define public space and does it exist as such in Beijing? Instead of simply focusing on physical spaces, I will try to capture some of the elements and the practices that make spaces public. Public space exists and changes as part of the urbanisation process, which is not simply material growth but also the means by which Beijingers learn how to deal with the anonymous "other". In this sense, I see public space as a subtle, unstable balance where public spaces express and shape the relationships between urbanites.

Josep Acebillo, ☞ page 14.

The metabolic analysis of urban

systems. Together with the shift from an industrial system to a neotertiary economy and with the globalization of decision-making processes, the irruption of new technologies forces us to envision an Urban Turn capable of creating a new Urban Complexity. Three directions can be foreseen to shape this new Urban Complexity: (1) a new concept of Urban Intensity, emphasizing interaction between urban density, urban granulometry and functional hybridity; (2) a revised notion of Urbanity, reinterpreting the symbiosis of urban identity and growing socio-cultural diversity; (3) a new Urban Metabolism able to sustainably process the flows of energy and materials which the city interchanges with the environment. This presentation addresses the last issue of the previous series, because in the light of the growing urbanisation of the planet, which can be seen in the fact that by the middle of this century some 70% percent of the population will live in cities, we have to seriously consider how many of the causes generating today's huge environmental crises—e.g. climate change—have their rationale in the metabolic inefficiency of our cities. Starting from the concept of urban metabolism, it is intended to analyze the conditions of urban metabolic efficiency while overcoming any form of simplistic and metaphorical analogy: greater metabolic efficiency will contribute to the rationalization of energy in urban system and to greater urban competitiveness. In order to achieve this goal, old arguments will be investigated while adopting new perspectives and a new hope—i.e. the influence which disruptive technologies have on new forms of urban mobility and therefore on energy issues. Urban metabolic analysis reveals the efficiency that small and medium-sized cities can have in the new neotertiary context, and it could be used as a test to evaluate in advance the functional and ecological consequences of future urban transformations.

research abstract

Paola Caputo, is an environmental engineer with a PhD in Energy Sciences. Since 2002 she has been a researcher at the Built Environment Science and Technology Dept. of the Politecnico di Milano. Since 1998 she has been collaborating with the Accademia di architettura in Mendrisio, where she coordinated the integrated SVC-EAD—Swiss Virtual Campus—Ecology in Architectural Design e-learning project and the UiSol—Urban Integrated Solar Systems project. From 1998 to 2001 she worked as a consultant for the Ambiente Italia Research Institute. From 2006 to 2009 she collaborated with SUPSI in Lugano in the field of energy and buildings. She has also worked for engineering and architectural firms on design processes. She has been member of international committees and has contributed to many national and international academic publications.

contribution to

research abstract

Energy and urban systems. The long, broad

debate on global environmental emergencies, population dynamics, energy-demand trends and the depletion of resources was recently stressed again also in the framework of the EU 20-20-20 energy package and subsequent targets for each EU country member. The importance of the role of the built environment and of urban energy systems has been underlined again, stressing the need for an energy revolution in order to change the present systems and trends towards more environmentally conscious, sustainable and renewable urban areas. Urban districts and communities represent an optimal scale for promising energy strategy implementation aimed at a more efficient use of energy and reduction in fossil fuel consumption, i.e. promoting the use of local renewable energies, distributed generation, micro-cogeneration and multi generation. However, apart from some particularly fortunate cases, there are still some barriers to be broken down in the infrastructural, economic, regulatory and political-administrative fields. To that end, one important gap to be filled is that of providing reliable models and applications in order to guide decisions concerning energy systems that limit the risk of dangerous errors and unpredictable negative effects. In order to achieve this, a suitable analysis of urban systems and an innovative survey and development of urban models, with the aim of fully understanding how urban metabolism can be improved, would be very appropriate and useful. The main aims of the USUM project are the definition of a useful notion of urban metabolism, the implementation of a methodology for assessing it, their application to the case studies of Lugano and Barcelona and the definition of guidelines for improving urban metabolism of cities with different characteristics and living conditions. At the heart of USUM WP1 is an analysis of the most significant energy and mass flows characterizing urban metabolism and their formal representation through a metabolic network. Data related to urban metabolism are collected and processed in order to evaluate suitable indicators to be brought together in a model that can provide a view of urban metabolism and of relative potential improvements, enlarging the evaluation to the most suitable aspects of the quality of life versus resources depletion and environmental problems. This model has been developed taking into account important research in which, despite the enormous complexity and diversity of human behaviour and extraordinary geographic variability as a metaphor, cities were modelled as organisms belonging to the same urban system governed by particular laws.

research abstract

Paolo Giordano, earned his PhD in Mathematics

from the University of Bonn. He has worked as a researcher for the European Community at the Institute of Applied Mathematics of the University of Bonn, and as director or co-director of several scientific projects for the EC, the Swiss National Science Foundation and the Cantonal administration. His main research interests are the mathematical modeling of complex systems, particularly with regard to applications in urban studies and transportation engineering, and the foundations of differential geometry using actual infinitesimals. At present he is a researcher at the University of Vienna and a lecturer at the Accademia di architettura in Mendrisio.

+

Alberto Vancheri, earned his PhD in Physics from

the University of Pavia. After teaching in high schools in Italy and Switzerland, he became a member of the Mathematics department at the Accademia di architettura in Mendrisio and currently teaches a course on the mathematical modeling of urban systems for MA students in Architecture. His research interests have evolved from theoretical and mathematical physics towards the applications of mathematics in the modeling of complex systems. His main focus is currently in the fields of urban dynamics (urban growth processes and housing markets), transport models, mathematical modeling of on-line communities and, more recently, the application of fuzzy systems to the assessment of urban efficiency.

Urban metabolism efficiency

indicators.

The USUM WP1is a first step towards a definition of a useful notion of urban metabolism and the implementation of a methodology for modeling and assessing it. More specifically, we introduce a method for the analysis of the most significant energy and mass flows characterizing urban metabolism based on a hierarchical organization and computation of the relevant variables. The hierarchical organization of the metabolic and metabolic-related variables mirrors the functioning of the urban system as a network of several subsystems: the transport subsystem, the built environment subsystem, and the socio-economic and cultural subsystem. From the mathematical point of view this hierarchical organization of knowledge and structures has been modeled through a hierarchical fuzzy inference system. This computational machinery produces a measure of the overall efficiency of an urban system, viewed as the capability of the system to be productive—in a broad sense, including economic production as well as quality of life—with the lowest possible environmental impact. An initial explorative application of this method has been accomplished using data about the cities of Lugano and Barcelona.

research abstract

Enrico Sassi, is an architect and teacher. He is a graduate of the Faculty of Architecture of the IUAV in Venice. He has collaborated with several architectural firms in Switzerland and Portugal. He has been the i.CUP—institute for Contemporary Urban Project coordinator and lecturer in Urban Design at the Accademia di architettura di Mendrisio since 2004-2005. In 2004-2005 he was head of the Planning and Information module of the Executive Master of Advanced Studies in Architecture program. In 2004-2005 he taught Architecture and Tourism in the Master of International Tourism program at the Faculty of Economics and Communication Sciences of the University of Lugano. Since 1998 he has been editor of the journal of architecture and urbanism Archi, the official organ of SIA, OTIA and ATEA. He edited the book "Guida alla storia del territorio" by Leonardo Benevolo.

+

Marc Montlleó Balsebre, started in 1997 as a junior consultant at Taller d'Enginyeria Ambiental. Since 1999, he has worked for the public agency Barcelona Regional, Metropolitan Agency for Urban Development and Infrastructures, in projects related to environmental and regional planning. At present, he is the director of Environmental Projects. He assisted Professor Richard T.T Forman for Barcelona Regional with the Greater Barcelona Land Mosaic and has participated in the Municipal Board of Sustainability of the Barcelona City Council and, representing the city council, has assisted the commission that follows the Air Quality Plan for the Barcelona area.

RESEARCH ABSTRACT

Urban metabolism case studies: comparing Barcelona and Lugano.

The USUM WP1 research mainly focuses on the urban system through the studies of what is called Urban Metabolism. The notion of Urban Metabolism is a biological way of looking at resource input and waste output of settlements, a basic metabolism concept that can be extended to include the dynamics of settlements, the economic strength and the livability of the settlement. Having stated this objective, we set out to study two specific cities: Barcelona and Lugano. Extremely different in term of dimensions and populations, these cities were chosen because of their paradigmatic representativeness and because of the availability of specific data: while Lugano represents an emblematic case of a small Swiss city, Barcelona is an emblematic case of a big European metropolitan system—for which the metropolitan development agency BCN Regional has been pivotal in supplying data. For research, access to data is a fundamental issue: even if data apparently always exists, often they are not available or not structured in a proper form, which proves how Urban Metabolism, even though extremely contemporary with respect to the debate on the sustainability of urbanisation processes, is still scarcely developed within the operative culture of territorial governance. In the specifics of these two cases, the majority of the data for the research have been specially calculated or extracted with specifically developed procedures. In the specifics, starting with a vast number of available data, a proposal has been advanced to analytically define and calculate what we consider to be the most crucial aspects of urban metabolism: CO_2 (annual CO_2 emissions, total and per capita); E (annual Energy consumption, total and per capita). The comparative method, requested by the development of the notion of urban metabolism within the USUM framework and applied to urban realities of different sizes, highlights a specific question of analytical methodology: the city can be an seen as a unitary system which expresses itself through an overall evaluation or as an assemblage which is expressed as the sum of its individuals. In other words the city can be conceptualized through absolute parameters (for which the scale is a determinant) or through relativized parameters (for which the scale is no longer meaningful). The analysis that we present in this presentation questions the limit between these two conceptualizations: the urban metabolism of cities with different sizes can be described and analyzed in order to highlight the specificities of every urban system and appropriately permit their comparison.

research abstract

Alessandro Martinelli, graduated in 2006 from the Accademia di architettura in Mendrisio with honors. In 2003 he founded AsMA—Association Making Architecture, an independent organization for research and communication in the field of contemporary architecture which in 2006 was awarded the OTIA—Order of Tessiner Architects award for an independent research about the profession of architecture in Europe. Since 2006 he has worked with i.CUP—institute for Contemporary Urban Project, at the Accademia di architettura in Mendrisio. From 2007 to 2009 he attended the Berlage Institute in Rotterdam. From 2009 to 2010 he took part in the USUM—Urban Systems and Urban Models research and he has been working as assistant tutor at the Berlage Institute on an annual research project on the relationship between spatial segregation and mass consumption in the form of tourism. In 2010 he also worked as an assistant professor for the Urban Studies course at the BiArch—Barcelona Institute of Architecture. Today he is a PhD candidate at the Accademia di architettura in Mendrisio while working as an independent architect and editor.

Urban metabolism and urban project.

Beyond the quantitative dimension, which is already significant in itself, the aspect that is most astonishing with respect to the current hypertrophic process of urbanisation is the progressive interrelation that is merging the world's urban spaces into what, with a certain degree of generalization regarding globalization processes, can be imagined as an enormous and progressively complex city swallowing the Earth. Growing complexity must now be accepted as the inevitable condition that accompanies any further human population development: the more numerous we are and the more we interconnect, the more the city will be complex. Nevertheless, if the experience of complexity, which pertains to a necessary evaluation of the limit of our autonomy, defines the system we live in, its emergence at the center of the urban question essentially confirms that the city ultimately "is" the system in which human beings take part. More precisely, if we cannot deny that we are biological organisms which need to continuously transform material and immaterial resources in order to maintain their life, we have to acknowledge how this system called the city must be first of all a biological one—which is to say a system where resources are negotiated through a continuous process of exchange, transformation and reuse, in which metabolic operations that dismantle and reconstitute these resources play a key role. Therefore, if the city is now the human biological system *par excellence*, I advance the idea that the urban space is now more than ever an environmental and cognitive device which mediates the complexity of that system, or rather a device which facilitates the metabolic connection of every one of us and the environment at large, from which we receive resources to be consumed, and towards which we deliver the resources we produce. More adequate coordination among production and consumption being a necessary objective in the light of the ecological and economic crisis in which we are embroiled today, the presentation advances the necessity to study, document and once again engage the urban project as an approach which deals with urban space—and today with urban metabolism therefore—from the most appropriate perspective, and that is the autonomy from where human beings advance their own projects and around which the very limit of complexity revolves.

Stanislava Boskovic Sigon, was born in
Bar, Montenegro, in 1977. She graduated in Architecture at the MArchI—Moscow Institute of Architecture in Russia, under Prof. Vyacheslav Glazychev, and obtained a Master in Advanced Studies in Territorial Architecture at the Accademia di architettura di Mendrisio in Switzerland, with Prof. Aurelio Galfetti. Since 2006 she has worked as an assistant to Prof. Josep Acebillo for the chair of Culture of Territory at the Accademia di architettura di Mendrisio. She worked as an assistant at the Faculty of Architecture of the Politecnico di Milano—Bovisa in Italy and at the Architectural Department of the University of Montenegro in Podgorica. She has cooperated with various architectural firms in Moscow, Milan, and Lugano. Since 2002 she has contributed to several architectural reviews in Moscow, Belgrade and Podgorica. She has coordinated and participated in various architectural seminars and festivals in Kazan, Moscow, and San Petersburg. Since 2007 she has taken part in the main international economic forums in Russia in Sochi and Krasnoyarsk. In 2007 she has founded the architectural office AUS—Architecture & Urban Systems while today she is PhD candidate at the Accademia di architettura di Mendrisio and partner of AS—Archtectural Systems office together with Josep Acebillo.

A metabolic reading of the post-Soviet city.

Since infrastructure constitutes a key device linking the metabolic processes of consumption and production, after the giant boom in the production of infrastructure and after the creation of the new Soviet state, Russia has proved to be, even just in terms of its quantitative dimension, an important case study to investigate, evaluate and engage with for a transposition of the metabolic paradigm in territorial studies at the planning level. Contemporary Russia is undergoing very dynamic and rapid development. Notwithstanding the fact that its economy clearly depends on the export of energy resources and raw materials, the Russian government has started an ambitious program of introducing new technologies and an innovation-based economy. This modernization, which positively affects both the social and the economic sphere, also has great impact on the territory and on the urban transformation of recent years. In light of this, it seems particularly interesting to offer an overview of the creation of Soviet cities in order to avoid possible problems and to underline all positive features of the impressive urban process that took place at the beginning of the Soviet Age. Since the disappearance of central planning, the Soviet city has found itself in radically different operating environments which, unlike the situation observed at the time of the Soviet Union, must now answer to novel relationships between the new theory of globalization, the neotertiary economy, and new technologies. While on the one hand the centralized state system is questioning the efficiency of the whole Russian territory, on the other hand the amazing extent of industrial and infrastructural resources constitutes a possible basis for grafting new technologies onto the territory and consequently stimulating its metabolic change. In all this process of creating an environment for innovation, which goes beyond the Government's intentions, in present-day Russia an important role is being played by the growing "business community", and educational and scientific institutions, advancing a new balance between public and private interests. The presentation will address how this environment under transformation today would again permit large scale projects, not only in Moscow but all over Russia, to be based on the existing urban legacy of the Soviet city and on new processes of innovation.

GLOBALIZATION OF URBANITY

Summer School final roundtable

Josep Acebillo, ☞ page 14.

+

Christian Schmid, ☞ page 50.

+

Jacques Levy, ☞ page 94.

+

Josep Lluis Mateo, since qualifying as an architect in 1974 and gaining his doctorate cum laude from the Universitat Politècnica de Catalunya in 1994, has always combined professional and academic activity. Since 2008, he has been the President of the Board of Directors of the BiArch—Barcelona Institute of Architecture and, since 2002, Professor of Architecture and Projects at the ETH Zurich. He has been a lecturer at numerous universities, and lectured and taught at the world's foremost institutions, including Princeton, Columbia University in New York, the Harvard Graduate School of Design, ABK Stuttgart, UP8 Paris, OAF Oslo and ITESM Mexico. He has also been Visiting Scholar at the Jean P. Getty Center in Los Angeles. With each of his projects, he seeks to connect the practice of construction with research and development in both intellectual and programmatic terms. He works in the area that brings together the sphere of ideas with the physical world of reality.

Researching Globalization of Urbanity.

Josep Lluis Mateo. Having following the works, I
would like to pose to each of you one question to point
out one specific aspect connected to your research.

The contemporary attraction for the informal city.

My first question is for Christian Schmid: the clearest
and quickest question I have after reading the papers
is related to the issue of "informality" and the research
being carried out on it. I would like to make a personal
vertical cross-section, which is historical in a way,
in terms of things connected to this issue. To me this
comes together with ideas from the 1950s and '60s,
like the book *Architecture without Architects* by Ber-
nard Rudofsky, with a preface by Louis Kahn, a book
that describes the architecture of the north of Africa
compared to contemporary forms. Kahn explains it

in its typically mystical way as the "truth" in its archaic original form, its "informality", as architecture out of the architects' world, and its archetypal resonance. This was also connected to discussions about the idea of the "exotic" and the "ethnic". Parallel to that there were some other kinds of "informality", related to the vernacular architectural paradigm, the "bon sauvage" described by Rousseau. Vernacular architecture was a kind of truth beyond architecture, beyond culture, like the real essence of something, with architects like Alvar Aalto and later Alvaro Siza and a whole generation of Spanish architects of the 50s. So, in your opinion, what might be the interesting aspects of these critical observations and research in our times?

Christian Schmid. I like the definition of "architecture without architects", which is what we discussed when we analyzed Mexico City and Kolkata, and the question about "informality". The crucial point is that many houses, especially in Mexico City, are really built without architects, and what you said about the pre-history of this situation is one of the main features of contemporary urbanisation processes. This not due to particular intentions but to poor local conditions: if you look at the actual speed of urbanisation processes even without going into great detail it is interesting to look at the sort of possibilities this architecture opens up: it is very flexible, for you can start with one floor and then add a second one, and you can just live there and maybe later even open a shop.
That's why I think this is really interesting and will become even more so in the future: it is certainly true that most architecture is built without architects.

Public space.

Josep Lluis Mateo. My second question is for Professor Lévy. This was the most difficult question for me because I only had a very small piece of text, and I had to imagine its content almost entirely from the title. Maybe it is the most banal thing: urban space and public space. It has certainly already been discussed but anyway repetition in another context can be good: as I see it, the problem of urban space comes from a contamination of its early origins. First, it seems to me that for many reasons public space is by definition connected with nostalgia. Urban space and public space is immediately connected to the idea of the square in Venice, Florence, La Rambla, Haussmannian boulevards and so on. It is a kind of status quo, which may or may not still be a reality. This is a kind of nostalgia for urban and public space, sometimes connected with a refusal of cars. But then urban space becomes a design problem: it seems that all over the world the square has to have special benches and lamps, transforming something that in my memory or in the past was more a structural piece into a furniture piece, an extension of the bench, a gigantic bench, with lamps, waste-paper baskets etc...

Jacques Lévy. I think we did not formulate public space like that! We agree instead with you: the problem with public space is not that it is an iconic expression, as European public space took shape in specifically material forms; on the contrary, the starting point for our reflection was that we have to think of the content, constructed as far as we can from its concrete expression, and we need to understand what a public space is. The problem is also to focus on the right present: we should not think that an urban space is necessarily free from cars, but we should also think of something beyond cars. This result is never achieved, so that is why in our first thesis we said that public space cannot be defined as a material space. We don't want to exclude architects and urban designers, and indeed we are thankful to them since we are financed by a

18 h 10 min

research program for architects, but the idea is that maybe when an architect has a proposal we have to raise the question that, in the making of a public space, all the actors, from politicians to citizens, have to be involved—experts but not only. Moreover, public space has a life cycle that is much longer than the designers' life, so in this case we have to invite to our table people who "are not there yet". I like Peter Sloterdijk's idea about globalization: he says that globalization is characterized by the fact that unilateral work has become impossible. He takes the case of Columbus and other great discoveries: once you put the flag of the king on a territory of a million hectares and just by this act this territory belongs to you. This would be impossible today because there are so many interactions and every actor has many feedbacks and he behaves differently from the way he would if he were alone. It is no coincidence that this connects with the notion of public space: we also have density in mind when we imagine how a public good, which is the public space, can be produced.

Organic versus Inorganic.

Josep Lluis Mateo. Thank you. So, here is my last question, which is for Professor Acebillo: actually it is more a statement that turns into a question. Professor Acebillo's research dealing with the idea of metabolism has been developed in recent times. First of all I would like to say that this idea is a kind of political possibility and in the end one of the main questions all over the world is how do we link it to economics, politics, and to citizens, and it is now part of the discussion on sustainability, ecology and energy, and is crucial in a good or bad way. There is a lot of discussion, especially in economics and at the social level, and it could be closely related to the problems of society. Taking care of these things in my opinion is crucial but one risk is that of taking it in a very technocratic and naive way, putting more machines into a building. The whole question of ecological sustainability and of energy consumption must therefore be carried out in a concise, cultural way. I think the idea of metabolism is a good tool for moving in this direction and it is much more than just a metaphor. This big "construction" is needed to intervene in the city. Metabolism could be addressed in a very real way, considering energetic fluxes or movements connected to biology: energy that is not created but just transformed and moving. But how is the idea of movement to be connected with immobility, and how is permanent organic motion connected to the fixed inorganic reality of architecture?

Josep Acebillo. Let me address it with a example: in this auditorium it is possible to host some hundreds of people, but if we start to envision to host here one thousand people, and it would be possible in relationship to the auditorium size, we will have first of all problems of stability, second it would be difficult to control the quality of air and its temperature, then the sound and so on. It is necessary to know the capacity of this auditorium in its overall complexity since, spurred by the apparent flexibility—what we could even understand as livability—of this space, the danger of putting here one thousand people is enormous.
When [Zygmunt] Bauman explains our society as mutated from a solid condition to a liquid one, it looks that the liquid one apparently doesn't need anything since it is very flexible and adaptable... Except for the fact that in any case its form is the form of its container, which means that in any case it depends on the relationship each time it unavoidably establishes with its context. In respect of these concerns, the idea of metabolism is not a metaphor. It is necessary to provide understanding of the material conditions of life to cities and to people who have responsibility for its governance.

And, especially questioning the necessity of social control for this kind of problems, I agree with you that movement—or rather life—is unavoidably paralleled by stability to unfold.

Switzerland.

Josep Lluis Mateo. Thank you very much. So we just go to the theme of advancing the research, talking about Swiss urban contemporary condition.

Christian Schmid. Well, we discussed a lot about different kinds of cities all over the world in the last two days, and in the end we came to Bellinzona. I think this will certainly help give us a better understanding of our present situation and also finding out more about Switzerland.
What is crucial for Switzerland is a specific contradiction, which has not been addressed at all in the past two days but which could be addressed in the future. On the one hand we still have considerable urban sprawl, despite all the discussions about urban density, centers of urbanity and public space. There is almost no slow-down in the process of urban sprawl and in the process of extending urban areas into the original landscapes in Switzerland. What is crucial is that we have certain amounts of these landscapes: they are limited and at a certain moment we are just consuming the last of these landscapes. They are used as a kind of extended garden, a *coulisse*, especially in the mountain areas and in the pre-Alps. In the long run this is a process that destroys not only the landscapes but also consumes the specific use-value of this space.
On the other hand we have a strong tendency towards concentration: there is an increasing demand for offices and housing in city areas, and it is also promoted by many planning instances that are calling for more density. However, density is increased precisely in these

areas that are already dense and that already have important urban qualities.

As a consequence, actual urbanisation in Switzerland implies a destruction of both qualities: on the one hand the qualities of the natural and cultural landscapes and on the other the destruction of urban qualities.

It would be interesting to have more research into these processes and this could also engage the concept of public space and metabolism in analyzing these processes.

Jacques Lévy. We will have to bring together all the methods of comparative analysis, urban structure, metabolism and public space: my starting point for the next stage will be a paradox, which is the fact that if you put Switzerland on a list of GDP per capita ranking at the European or world level, its position is excellent. But if you look at urban Switzerland, it is quite different. You can compare for instance the whole of Switzerland to other configurations of 8 million people and, from recent studies, we see that Paris, for instance, has a GDP which is almost double that of Switzerland, even though France as a whole is much poorer that Switzerland; if you look at Basel or Zurich, the richest cities in Switzerland, there is a GDP much smaller than that of Paris or London. So, this prompts me to suggest that we could analyze different spatial configurations inside Switzerland, without prejudices about the most relevant and efficient ones. For instance we could study a city, a metropolis in Switzerland, but also a place which is not supposed to be a city but nonetheless is an urban space, as the *Urban Portrait* [by Christian Schmid] showed, to see which are the most efficient configurations, and maybe we will find some surprises. I do not have the right answer yet but we have to use our methodology to make improvements, to propose something which could act as a sort of spatial configuration, bench-marking inside Switzerland; of course we can also look outside, to see which are the best economic configurations, not only economically, but also in terms of ecological efficiency. This could be the useful part of our work, because we are carrying out our research and education among PhD students, but we could also be of some use to society. It could be interesting because I think Switzerland is facing new challenges in terms of innovation, of rearrangements within society in order to respond to what will be our productivity tools, like innovation, creation, things that are not necessarily those that assured the prosperity of today's Switzerland, which could be different in the near future. What would be the right configuration for the new development of Switzerland? We might try to answer this question.

Josep Acebillo. When I started working in this question about metabolism, 4 or 5 years ago, I was already thinking in terms of territory. I have been in America many times, and I have always been staying in New-York, in Chicago or in Los Angeles. From there I was used to take a car and visit all around, from St. Louis to Amarillo and I'm telling you this since in the States it is simply impossible to move with other means of transportation. So, it is true that in Switzerland there is a strong presence of sprawl, but I think there are some particular conditions to it: the first is that the Swiss sprawl is different from the sprawl of the rest of the world. It is not similar to the American sprawl, where it expresses the will to live as close as possible to the nature: this is not the sprawl that you can find in Catalonia, in Spain or in other Mediterranean countries. In Switzerland, from the metabolic point of view, it doesn't exist a very strong difference between the cities and the countryside. Here in Switzerland there are transitions in the territory that are to me very interesting, in the sense that little by little you approach a city as it was through a garden. But when you cross America, or

18 h 40 min

when you go in Russia from St. Petersburg to Moscow,
there is a strong contrast between agriculture, heavy
industries and the city centers. This contrast doesn't exist
in Switzerland and it is important to keep it in mind.
In this respect, I would like to address in the second
part of the work the possibility to transform the existing
Swiss sprawl into an urban network. It is not impossible.
Why I do think so? Because the essential difference
between the Swiss sprawl and the American one is
that you have a very rich infrastructure for mobility. In
this sense my answer turns into a question: why are we
abandoning the "Swiss Metro" idea? I suppose that
there are political reasons and economical ones and so
on, but this project was perfect to suit both the territorial
structure, and the topology of Switzerland.
In this sense I think that one problem of today's Switzerland is that it lost the innovative character that it had in
the nineteenth century, when the first railway network
was here developed, the first tunnels as well... Notwithstanding this, I see here the possibility to discover
new urban typologies, especially when we address the
"regional city idea". It would be not possible of course
here to fully inquiry what I call the "archipelago" model
but for many reasons my interest in the second phase
of this project has to do precisely with the specific-ness
of the Swiss reality.

GLOBALIZATION OF URBANITY

Summer School excursus

excursus

The following conversation is a by product of the Globalization of Urbanity Summer School and involved Neil Brenner, ☞ **page 78**, interviewed by Alessandro Martinelli, ☞ **page 140**, with Guillermo Delgado and Philip Luhl, Summer School participants.

Globalization of Urbanity afterthoughts...
a conversation with Neil Brenner.

Alessandro Martinelli. Can you give us a statement on the issue of globalization of urbanity from your perspective as a sociologist and geographer who has written extensively on neoliberalism and related issues?

Neil Brenner. Globalization is a term that has been used quite a bit in social theory during the last decades. Many scholars, myself included, have adopted the term as a way to critique state-centric approaches to social science, inherited from postwar social science and subsequently naturalized within the mainstream disciplinary division of labour, which presuppose that social relations are territorially enclosed within national boundaries. As a graduate student at the University of Chicago in the mid-1990s, I got interested in globalization studies in part because I wanted to break out of this state-centric or methodologically territorialist approach to the social sciences. In that context, it was very productive to read the writings of scholars such as Immanuel Wallerstein and Saskia Sassen and, more generally, to engage with the globalization debates, especially in critical geography and critical geopolitical economy. At that time, as Peter Taylor once remarked, those debates really entailed an effort to "open up new spaces" for social-theoretical analysis-questions of scale, place and territory could thus be opened up for social-scientific analysis rather than being seen as pregiven dimensions of political-economic life.

But more recently, however, I've become much more critical of the globalization debates and even of the term globalization itself. For instance, these days the term globalization has become something of a chaotic concept—it's so generic and imprecise that it's often used without any analytic content, that is, to refer to a rather disparate set of phenomena and transformations that may only be contingently linked to one another. The term thus becomes a general way of describing contemporary worldwide social change-and, as such, almost meaningless. A related, and equally serious problem is that the term globalization is often used to construct a despatialized, deeply ideological model of social processes, what Castells has famously called "the space of flows". The idea here is of seamless integration of social relations across the world—the "end of geography" or the dissolution of territory. But this vision of contemporary capitalism is seriously flawed since it generalizes one dimension of contemporary sociospatial processes-flow, circulation, networks-into a metaphor for the totality. This is a dangerous and misleading analytical move since, as urbanists such as ourselves have argued, the intensified flow and circulation of commodities, capital and labour necessarily presupposes fixed and immobile spatial infrastructures that are territo-

Neil Brenner, Alessandro Martinelli, Guillermo Delgado, Philip Luhl

rialized, scaled and placed in historically specific ways. This is, of course, an argument David Harvey made long ago regarding the urban process under capitalism, and I would argue that it continues to provide a powerful counterpoint to some of the ideologies of neoliberal globalization that remain popular today.

Consequently, these days, instead of using the word "globalization" I prefer to just talk about "global restructuring", which refers to the worldwide scale and to the idea that there's a restructuring process going on, which then has to be specified both substantively and spatially.

Alessandro Martinelli. What do you think is the duty of your discipline with regard to such processes?

Neil Brenner. I don't really identify my intellectual project with any singular discipline in the social sciences or beyond: the questions we are discussing here are really interdisciplinary if not post-disciplinary. In a way, the disciplinary division of labour is inherited from a state-centric model. The disciplinary division of labour emerged in the early twentieth century and it was consolidated in the mid-twentieth century. The idea was that each nation state had a society, an economy, a culture and a state; therefore you had sociology, economics, political science and anthropology. Arguably, contemporary patterns of global restructuring have totally exploded that way of organizing our epistemology of the world, necessitating new forms of investigation and analysis, new methods and new cartographies of social space. Of course, there are disciplinary responses to contemporary debates on global restructuring: for example, sociology or political science or geography may try to develop a particular way of dealing with contemporary transformations, claiming that its method or its object of analysis is distinctive. Indeed, there is an orthodox response that tries to use inherited disciplinary tools to grapple with these new realities. Personally, though, I have always rejected the disciplinary division of labour. With all due respect to our colleagues who identify their work with a particular discipline, I have just never found it to be a productive way of thinking about cities, about urbanisation, about globalization, or about regulatory change. Obviously, insofar as universities are organized according to the disciplinary division of faculties, we cannot ignore the disciplines: we teach classes and grant degrees within disciplines, but nonetheless we can use the pedagogy of teaching and research to advance a critique of these disciplines. Ultimately, whatever insights may be facilitated through specialization, disciplines may also come to constrain knowledge: they impose arbitrary limits on the kinds of questions we have been debating in this conference. The world, simply put, is not divided into disciplines, so neither should our modes of investigation, especially in the contemporary period.

Alessandro Martinelli. In any case we have seen today how difficult it is to find some kind of interdisciplinary ground. Architects ask of course how we do urbanisation, rather like the way Christian Schmid was asking how we represent urbanisation, which is a totally different thing. It is not even disciplinary, and in the end it is very hard to find space for debate, especially if you want to be critical.

Neil Brenner. Yes, indeed, these are very difficult issues, but it is hugely important, in my opinion, to grapple with them patiently, thoroughly and systematically. If people have totally different concerns and totally different categories and totally different epistemologies, then in such conversations people would just throw up their arms in frustration and give up on communication entirely. But, as we have seen in this conference, there are a lot of shared concerns among scholars and practitioners trained in very different fields, and even if translation is not easy, it often generates very fruitful insights that would not be possible if participants were to remain within their usual intellectual 'comfort zones.' For instance, as a social scientist and urban theorist, I have always benefited immensely from conversations with architects: our methods may differ, but many concerns are shared. What is the broader political-economic context in which buildings are constructed, and how is the building or site articulated to the broader urban fabric, at various scales stretching from the local and the regional to the national and even the global? From my point of view the fundamental question is whether individuals from different disciplines have shared concerns and shared questions. If they do there is always a possibility for dialogue, even if it often entails having to work together intensively to develop a shared vocabulary and to understand the implications of different methodological and conceptual choices for analysis, and indeed, for practice. Such an effort presupposes openness and patience on both sides, but it can generate surprising and productive results-consider, for example, Christian Schmid's remarkable collaboration with his architect colleagues in Studio Basel in their path-breaking book, *Switzerland—An Urban Portrait.*

Alessandro Martinelli. In any case the processes of urbanisation are something which is happening in specific spaces and times and which is therefore not the same in a month's or a year's time. There is a progressive speed in the transformation of urbanisation processes that unfortunately is not rivaled by studies and research speed; knowledge is not developing so fast, and the interdisciplinary one, with all of its need to debate, even less. As a consequence, the interdisciplinary need turns to be a paradox in front of the progressive speed of mutation of urbanisation processes. In the light of this apparent aporia, should we radically envision a new approach, a new epistemological paradigm?

Neil Brenner. We need to be aware, as experts, of inherited traditions of twentieth century urban studies. We need to understand these traditions, their epistemologies, the key debates of the field during the last century; only then can we even begin to consider how to transcend them. On the other side, I also like the idea of pursuing "a fresh start", of developing a radically new kind of approach. I think that is a very fundamental impulse, and we need more of these impulses-a willingness to take some risks, to undertake rather ambitious conceptual and methodological experiments. Too much of contemporary urban studies presupposes an inherited research paradigm-what Thomas Kuhn long ago called "normal science"—rather than trying to explode the paradigm. A new paradigm, or at least new approaches, can begin emerge because certain old questions can no longer be answered within existing frameworks. Once you start to reform those research paradigms, entirely new questions emerge that could not even be envisioned within previous frameworks. This kind of paradigm-transforming work is as important, from my point of view, as concrete research on a neighbourhood or on a city. Both types of work are, of course, interconnected. You need a theory to guide your research, but at the same time the most revolutionary research entails trying to explode, or at least pushing the boundaries of the very theory that it is guided by. That process never ends; we are never going to find the "correct" theory— there's no such thing because we're living in a urbanizing world that is constantly being creatively destroyed.

Guillermo Delgado. I think it is pertinent to refer to Henri Lefebvre, since the presentation given by Christian Schmid just addressed his work, and, furthermore, since Lefebvre surely left a changed paradigm with his work. In any case, he didn't propose a methodology but rather a series of questions. In your lecture as well there was an amazing moment in which in the same way as

Proudhon asked "what is property?" and Marx asked "what is money?", you came and asked "what is the city?". It was a moment that disarmed some of us, and left open the possibility to consider that it could very well be a project.

Neil Brenner. This is indeed one of my central concerns-what happens to the field of 'urban' studies when the category of the 'city' is superseded through urbanisation processes? I gave a lecture in the series of conferences that Christian [Schmid] and Lukasz [Stanek] were organizing on Henri Lefebvre in Zurich and in Delft. My contribution to the November 2009 conference was a paper titled "The Field Formerly Known as Urban Studies," and it basically argued that the city is an ideology, just as the notion of the nation is an ideology. For me, and indeed building strongly on Lefebvre's work, the underlying forces must be understood in terms of urbanisation, not in terms of the city (or any other fixed 'unit' of settlement space). Once you make that move, if you look back at the history of twentieth century urban studies, you suddenly have to break quite radically with a lot of the epistemological assumptions that have underpinned the field, certainly since the interventions of the Chicago School in the 1920s, possibly even earlier. Because the field has been constructed around the idea that its purpose is to study a particular kind of settlement space, namely the city, exploding this-reference point entails a radical destabilization. What remains of 'urban' studies after making such a radical move? This is a matter for future debate, but my own view is that the field's object should be the process, the churning, the creative destruction, of settlement spaces across the uneven landscapes of capitalism, encompassing all those zones that were once categorized as 'city', 'suburban', 'rural' and so forth. Such terms—the rural, the city, the countryside, the metropolitan, the regional, the suburban—all are expressions of underlying social processes that generate the illusion that space has a certain fixity. This is, however, illusory: under capitalism there is constant change, not least in patterns and landscapes of sociospatial organization. We need to focus on the processes that generate change, rather than the temporary, often ideological, expressions of that change.

Philip Luhl. I could even refer to Marx defining the city in *Capital* as it is the place that is required for the division of labour, and that it also has a lot to do with density, of course, but density not as an absolute condition rather depending on what he calls the Verkehrsmittel ["mode of transport"]. So he is saying that a non-dense space in terms of absolute density can actually become dense in terms of social relations or in terms of relations of production. That already includes the possibility not to see the city as the object enclosed but something that essentially relates to other things.

Neil Brenner. Yes, exactly, space is a profoundly relational concept in Marx, and their are hidden gems of insight in volume 2 of *Capital* that have yet to be properly excavated for considering such issues. Another interesting passage pushing in a similar direction is in the *Communist Manifesto*, when Marx and Engels talk about the ways in which capitalism has liberated the countryside from "the idiocy of rural life". As it turns out, for Marx and Engels, the word Idiotie does not mean stupidity, but is derived from a particular Greek word, whose connotation would have been clear to them, meaning "isolation from the community," or "being disconnected from political life". So this formulation is not, in fact, an anti-rural screed, but actually entails a substantive claim about capitalism's effect on spatial organization: it creates intense, expanding connectivity between different places and scales, and thus its opposite, "idiocy" simply connotes disconnectedness, not stupidity. On this reading, then, the rural is defined as an enclave that is separated out from exchange, from interaction, whereas the urban is simply a condition of intense connectedness, regardless of what spatial morphology that connectedness may assume. I may be imposing my own interests upon the *Communist Manifesto*, here, but I don't think it's implausible to view this famous passage as a starting point for theorizing about our contemporary condition of generalized or "planetary" urbanisation.

Alessandro Martinelli, ☞ page 140.

Editor's note

Confronted with the multifaceted and very diverse materials appearing in these proceedings—which reflect the current fragmentation of urban studies—I think the duty of an editor engaging in such a field is not only to highlight the differences, in order to distinguish the various disciplinary positions, but also to offer hope for the possibility of certain continuities along the various approaches. And it does not matter if these continuities are generic since, precisely because of such genericness, they could hint at conditions inherent in the hegemonic character that the processes of urbanisation and globalization have acquired today.

What I aim to do here and throughout the pages of these proceedings is therefore to highlight at least one point that all the presentations seem to share, and consequently to offer a temporary, or at least provisional, canvas to host their differences.

One of the potential "attractors" of the discourses about urbanisation and globalization here collected is the progressive *plea for an understanding of the city as the manifestation of real-time evolving processes.* From this perspective, urbanisation and globalization seem to force us to consider the necessity to mutate the idea of the city from being an object—with a covertly institutional status—to a procedural entity.

(☞ page 165)

If we consider that, according to Andrea Cavalletti, Ildefons Cerdà essentially *turned the city into a process* while establishing the first projective definition of urbanisation in his 1850s *General Theory of Urbanisation*, we could even argue that the very idea of urbanisation has its roots in this proceduralization of the inhabitable world. In fact, the project of urbanisation applied to an existing city *"does not mean modern expansion as the enlargement of urban space, but rather its turning into a process; what is at stake is a continuous and unitary flow according to which even the smallest house becomes the elemental and original urbe."* (☞ page 173, Reference1)

But this proceduralization must not be understood as the destabilizing liquefaction of a previous solid system, as certain well-known authors have advanced in the past two or three decades, rather looks to be the *relativization of life to specific inhabitable conditions,* or the understanding of the territory as the emergent co-presence of "fixities and motions", to use Neil Brenner's definition (☞ Ref.2) here quoted by Christian Schmid, in continuous interaction and interdependence.

(☞ page 66)

The necessity to understand the city in its dynamic processes has in fact corresponded a parallel need to acknowledge the spatio-temporal conditionality of life (☞ Ref.3), that is the fact for which life in any case takes place in real times and real spaces, by necessity implying a spatio-temporal context—a certain conditional fixity—to host all the motions it involves.

In a way we can therefore argue that, in the last two centuries, the absolute idea of *living* has been progressively superseded by a conditional idea of *inhabiting a context,* which essentially means that, as living entities, we have been progressively facing the question of our unavoid-

Alessandro Martinelli

able *system condition*, or the fact that in order to survive in our biological autonomy we need to develop, manage and maintain a certain set of crucial relationships with the environmental as well as social context that surround us. (☞ Ref.4)

The mankind development sustainability question is finally opening the way for such acknowledgement of the human *system condition*; not by chance the establishment of the contemporary definition of world urbanisation sustainability coincided with the famous UN's Brundtland commission declaration of *systemic threat*: "*The Earth is one but the world is not. We all depend on one biosphere for sustaining our lives. Yet each community, each country, strives for survival and prosperity with little regard for its impact on others.*" (☞ Ref.5) In other words, if today we are finally forced to realize our *system condition*, it is becasue the *emergent actuality of our system finitude*, channeled through the worldwide networks of our globalized urbanity, makes it an inescapable context to human life.

Such inescapable *system condition* then brings with itself a relevant corollary: its confrontation with the constant demand for growth that mankind keeps advancing will progressively force any further development of ours to essentially happen in the form of a *system differentiation*. Unfortunately, this experience-able transformation of the system in which we take part is already trying out our finite capacities for management and gradually exposing us to the impossibility of unilateral action —as Jacques Levy has stated—or, in other words, to the cognitive complexities of *cohabitation*, that is to inhabit together with what is different from us.

(☞ page 150)

This impossibility leads therefore to a general and shared plea for a new epistemology - or, more precisely, for a renewed cognitive economy of what I would consider a *system epistemology* - which stops considering any object independently from the systemic relations that this interweaves with its context. We essentially need to search for new cognitive tools that, while offering us the possibility of system complexity *synthesis*, could

171

permit an overall economy of the actions needed for managing and maintaining our systemic development throughout space and time. And such a research for proper cognitive tools is extremely urgent since their absence could be understood as the very reason why our public administrations are progressively wasting energies precisely trying to face the question of how to manage and to maintain our systemic development, that

(☞ page 34) is what Josep Acebillo has framed as the administrative question of *glocalization*.

in the light of this plea for proper cognitive tools, I think we need to rediscover what is the *possibility for order*, beyond its misleading acceptation of regimentation. If we accept that - as Michel Foucault has already advanced many years ago (☞ Ref.6) - absolute freedom doesn't exist but it is rather something that must be exercised, that is the fact - as I have already outlined - for which anything takes place along with its systemic relationship with a context, the construction of the *possibility for order*, preserving the relative autonomy of system parts while offering the possibility of their relational *synthesis*, looks not to be a matter of regimentation but rather the vital exercise of a possible emancipation: in systemic terms, such construction opens a space for an economy of management and maintenance that is the very essence both of order and sustainability.

According to Ludwig Hilberseimer, whose late theoretical works had a prophetic appeal in spite of their post-modern misfortunes, "*Order is an organic process. It should not be mistaken for organization, which is a mechanical one. Order deals with life as well as with the forms and means of life. [..] Order grows out of the nature of things [..] and relates the part to the whole and the whole to the parts. [..] Order provides the medium in which everything can grow and unfold.*" (☞ Ref.7) Accepting the *system condition* of all things, the *possibility for order* looks to be what offers space and time for the existing as well as for the unprecedented.

Alessandro Martinelli

Besides what would look like an apparent banality in terms of scientific research, a quest for the *possibility for order* is what in my opinion emerges from the fragmentation of urban studies but, paradoxically, unitary plea for comparison as an operative tool: whatever we want to call it - the possibility for a new form of urban theory, for urban comparison, for a projective notion of urban / public space... - we-global-urbanites hope in the *possibility for order*.

Precisely because it doesn't rely on totalizing narratives or naïve morality, the "Globalization of urbanity" proceedings is a sincere manifestation not of the specificity of urban studies but rather of the systemic character—I don't call it generic anymore—of the concerns that contemporary urbanity poses.
In front of the "Globalization of urbanity" Summer School reality, with all of its systemic complexities, the possibility for order is here the responsibility of a designed graphic structure that, with an overabundant set of indexes, situates any of the proceedings parts with respect to the research structure which has generated its content, to the Summer School which has delivered it, and to the actual "thickness" of the book containing them.

References
1. Cavalletti, A. (2005), *La città biopolitica, Mitologie della sicurezza*. Milano: Paravia Bruno Mondadori. page 22—23 (translation by the author).
2. Brenner, N. (2000), Between fixity and motion: accumulation, territorial organization and the historical geography of spatial scales. In *Environmental and Planning Digest: Society and Space* 16.
3. I refer with such comment to the plea for a general re-embedding of res extensa into being as advanced by Latour, B. (2009), Spheres and networks: two ways to reinterpret globalization. In *Harvard Design Magazine* 30.
4. Such understanding of system as depending on the maintenance of relationship has been scientifically drafted in the General System Theory and especially through the open systems rationale: Bertalanffy, L. v. (2004), *Teoria generale dei sistemi: fondamenti, sviluppo, applicazioni* (E. Bellone, Trans.). Milano: Mondadori.
5. UN Brundtland commission (1987), *Our Common Future—A Threatened Future*. Oxford: UN. chapter. 1 art. 1.
6. Foucault, M., (2001), Space, Knowledge and Power, In Rabinow, P. et al., *The essential works of Michel Foucault*. London: Penguin.
7. Hilberseimer, L. (1949), *The new regional pattern: industries and gardens, workshops and farms*. Chicago: Paul Theobald.

Editor's note

Author:
**Josep Acebillo, Jacques Levy,
Christian Schmid, et al.**

Published by:
**Accademia di architettura - USI
(Università della Svizzera italiana),
Mendrisio CH
and ACTAR**

Edited by:
Alessandro Martinelli
(www.as-ma.org)

Editorial assistant:
Marco Capitanio

Graphic design & Production:
ActarPro

Printed and bound
in the European Union

ISBN: 978-84-92861-81-1
DL: B-14368-2012

Distribución
ActarD
Barcelona—New York
www.actar-d.com

Roca i Batlle 2
E-08023 Barcelona
T +34 93 417 49 93
F +34 93 418 67 07
salesbarcelona@actar.com

151 Grand Street, 5th floor
New York, NY 10013, USA
T +1 212 966 2207
F +1 212 966 2214
salesnewyork@actar.com

Images & Photographs:

Courtesy of **Barcelona Regional
Metropolitan Agency**
page 22, 28

Courtesy of **Josep Acebillo**
page 36

Courtesy of **NASA/Goddard Space
Flight Center, Scientific Visualization
Studio**
page 70

Courtesy of **Christian Schmid,
Switzerland - An Urban Portrait
research**
page 60, 62, 64

Courtesy of **Christian Schmid,
Urban Systems and Urban Models
research**
page 72

Courtesy of **Jacques Levy**
page 98, 102, 106

Swiss Cooperation Programme in Architecture
USUM - Urban Systems and Urban Models

Marcello Martinoni
USUM coordinator - secretary

-

Josep Acebillo
USUM - Working Package 1 responsible

Enrico Sassi
Paola Caputo
Paolo Giordano
Alberto Vancheri
Gian Paolo Torricelli
Elena Molteni
Stanislava Boskovic Sigon
Simone Garlandini
Alessandro Martinelli
USUM - Working Package 1 research group
Urban metabolism studies as global urbanisation agenda

-

Christian Schmid
USUM - Working Package 2 responsible

Pascal Kallenberger
Anne Schmidt
Monika Streule
USUM - Working Package 2 research group
Patterns and pathways of global urbanisation

-

Jacques Lévy
USUM - Working Package 3 responsible

Gian Paolo Torricelli
Véronique Mauron
Monique Ruzicka-Rossier
Annelore Schneider webmaster
Paolo Dos Santos Student assistant - web
Frédéric Gökçiyel Student assistant - social sciences
USUM - Working Package 3 research group
Urban / public spaces in the global urbanisation era

For information, please contact i.CUP - institute for Contemporary Urban Project,
Accademia di architettura, Università della Svizzera Italiana - Largo Bernasconi 2, 6850
Mendrisio, Switzerland - tel. +41 58 6665980 - fax. +41 58 6665813 - icup@arch.unisi.ch